Clare Harman Clark is a Senior Counsel – Knowledge in the real estate team at Taylor Wessing LLP. She chairs the Property Section at the Law Society and teaches on the *Property Law and Practice* and *Commercial Property* modules of the LPC at the University of Westminster.

Back in the mists of time, she trained as a journalist and still writes regularly for national and trade press. She sits on the editorial board of the Landlord and Tenant Review and has contributed chapters to various books on the development of legal practice (including *Career Development for Women Lawyers*; *Tomorrow's KM: innovation, best practice, and the future of knowledge management*; and *Lawyer's guide to the future of practice management*).

Since qualifying at Clifford Chance LLP, she has spent the best part of two decades advising on all aspects of commercial real estate, for a vast array of clients. In her current role, Clare focuses on knowledge management and enjoys the professional space to leverage her transactional experience while engaging with the macro trends affecting our sector. She recently completed a Masters in International Planning and Sustainable Development – for all the discussion on pandemics, or Brexit, or technology, by far the biggest issue facing us today is the climate change crisis.

# A Practical Guide to Green Leases for Property Professionals

# A Practical Guide to Green Leases for Property Professionals

Clare Harman Clark

Law Brief Publishing

Published 2023 by Law Brief Publishing, an imprint of Law Brief Publishing Ltd
30 The Parks
Minehead
Somerset
TA24 8BT

www.lawbriefpublishing.com

Paperback: 978-1-916698-24-6

# PREFACE

Green leasing has the capacity to drive fundamental change in the real estate sector, but to do so impactfully it must be met by ambitious investors and owners, and driven by real estate practitioners who understand and support its aims.

Heartfelt thanks to Tim, Nate, Ollie and Tess for providing the most compelling reason for change. Thank you, Tor, for reminding me when to take a break. Thank you, Alison, who planted the seeds of curiosity and challenge many moons ago. Your scientific expertise was much appreciated Tim Scarbrough. And thank you, Nanna. Women could not even be lawyers when you were born but without your encouragement and belief, I wouldn't be one now.

I'm endlessly grateful to be surrounded now by some incredible, knowledgeable and committed colleagues at both Taylor Wessing (including Daniel Hirschfield, Annabel Pyke and Lorraine Smith) and the Law Society (including Warren Gorden, Alasdair Cameron and Andrew Wiseman). Without their generous patience and guidance, writing this would have been considerably less enjoyable.

Lastly, particular thanks to Josh van den Dries of The Chancery Lane Project and Laura Noctor-King of the Better Buildings Partnership. I really appreciated you taking the time to support this project. And I'm convinced the subject matter of the book, and your passion for collaborative development behind the scenes, will not only stand the test of time in the commercial real estate world but also redefine it.

The law and practice described in this book is far reaching and fast changing, but it is correct at the conclusion of editing, on 22nd October 2023.

*Clare Harman Clark*
*October 2023*

# CONTENTS

# CHAPTER ONE

# INTRODUCTION – CHANGING THE WORLD

"*Change the precedent, change the world.*"[1]

And the fact is the world needs changing.

Since the dawn of time, the world's climate has been continually in flux but the enormous, existential threat of human influence on that natural variation is now established fact. There is a legitimacy of consensus between environmental scientists, conservation groups and green activists throughout the globe: the climate is changing and the *rate* of warming challenges life as we know it. In the last century or so, since trackers have been able to obtain reliable data for baseline comparison, we have collectively, and dramatically, hiked average global surface temperatures. At the time of writing, new records for daily temperature anomalies (i.e. departures from the meteorological norm) peaked at around 1.9°C higher than the so-called "pre-industrial" levels of 1850-1900.[2] Yet since the Intergovernmental Panel on Climate Change (IPCC) released its Fifth Assessment report on 2 November 2014, it's been widely understood that an average increase must be kept to an absolute maximum of 1.5°C. This is the aspirational goal of the United Nation's November 2016 Paris Agreement, and sits at the heart of many science-based targets (SBTs) for climate action (more on drafting these in **Chapter 4**). There is a clarion call is for genuinely effective action.

1 This quote is from Matthew Gingell, GC of Oxygen House Group and the founder and chair of TCLP, who was speaking at the TCLP Plenary Session (2nd Annual Hackathon) on 5 November 2020.

2 Hausfather, 29 September 2023.

Understanding the nuances of the crisis and its ultimate impact can be extremely challenging; scientific literature is dense and technical. Still, the world's climate scientists (including those at the IPCC) make predictions using the relatively accessible Representative Concentration Pathways (RCPs) tool. RCPs are not a strict measure of emissions per se, but they make assumptions about atmospheric greenhouse gas (GHG) concentration in our atmosphere and build remarkably visual models for policy makers, which consider rising temperatures in the context of possible adaption and mitigation strategies. Depending on the volume of GHG emitted in the years to come, they set out a series of different pathways to possible futures in 2100, each relative to that earlier, nineteenth century world.

Each RCP scenario is named in relation to targets for atmospheric radiation, expressed in watts per square metre. And each exhibits socio-economic assumptions relating to our technology, economy and population trajectories, making very real what *could* come to pass. Towards the more hopeful end of the potential climate change spectrum is the RCP 2.6 scenario, which should keep the best estimate of global average temperature rise to 1.6 °C by 2090-2100. But it is a "very stringent" pathway that requires GHG emissions to decline dramatically from 2020 and reach zero by the end of the century. The intermediate pathway of RCP 3.4 meanwhile includes the considerable removal of GHG, but still leaves mean global warming of up to 2.4°C by 2100.

If we cannot, collectively, put into place effective, protective climate policies, RCP 4.5 sees GHG emissions peak around 2040. These will then decline, thanks ultimately to the exhaustible character of non-renewable fuels, but more likely than not we will face a global temperature rise of 2-3 °C by 2100, and a mean sea level rise 35% higher than that in RCP 2.6. Many plant and animal species are unlikely to be able to adapt to the effects of RCP 4.5.

Across each RCP pathway, the picture for the late 21st century is concerning. In aggregate, they project a global mean temperature rise of between 0.3°C and 4.8 °C, with global mean sea level rise of between

0.26m and 0.82m. Towards the (even more) worrying end of the RCP spectrum, RCP 6 sees emissions peak around 2080. They will then decline thanks to technologies and strategies, but by 2100 global temperatures will still be up by 3–4 °C (i.e. at least double the maximum IPCC target). The best basis for our *worst-case* climate change scenario is RCP 8.5. Here, emissions continue to rise unmitigated throughout the 21st century, leading to a global average temperature rise of 4.3°C by 2100. RCP 8.5 is often used to predict a "very high baseline emission scenario": what could happen, in the worst case, where no effective policies are put in place.

Ultimately, expect huge and unprecedented consequences on our personal and business lives. On a global scale, the World Economic Forum's Global Risk Report 2022 listed climate action failure, extreme weather and biodiversity loss as the three most severe risks of the next decade. Closer to home, in July 2020, the UK's Met Office recorded a mock weather forecast for 2050, based on that high emissions scenario. A serious meteorologist looks into the camera: "Do what you can to stay cool [...] the most severe heat warning is currently in force." The same scientist offers a debrief after the forecast: "Now *possible* and *could* are words that express uncertainly, but don't let that lull you into a false sense of security." The message was clear. Business as usual mean we can expect multiple days of extreme heat; record breaking temperatures; high alerts for wildfires, storms and drought. *Apocalyptic* weather. Inevitable breakdowns in infrastructure, communications and homes.

No doubt since before Cassandra's curse, polite society has dismissed doomsayers. But even a cursory recent glance at genuine weather reports suggests the Met Office's dramatic high emissions scenario is already manifest, a generation ahead of time. 2023 brought the warmest summer *ever* reported in the northern hemisphere. When the world's average temperature reached a new high on Monday 3 July 2023, it topped "17 degrees Celsius for the first time. [...T]the highest in any instrumental record dating back to the end of the 19th century."[3] The Guardian quoted climate scientist Friederike Otto, of London's Grantham Institute for Climate Change and the Environment, who called the heat "a death sentence for people and ecosystems." And it was squarely blamed on climate change.

## Shifting the dial

There is a compelling argument that the country's future growth and prosperity depends on pivoting its entire economy towards the green revolution, just as it has pivoted in the past from agrarian to manufacturing, to services professions. In the long term, renewable energy must be manifestly cheaper and more sustainable than fossil fuels. We can of course debate the pace of change. We can balance the politic of measured contributions and personal sacrifices against the demands of a climate *emergency* that would dictate shifts virtually overnight, like wartime industrial pivots. It doesn't really matter: either way, whole sectors need to be equipped with clear strategy and policy to have the confidence to invest for the challenge, attract capital and serve communities, however the challenge will be faced.

When it comes to tangible national leadership in this climate change battle then, we will explore in Chapter 2 how, together, the existing statutes, regulations and policies constitute a rather flimsy and frustratingly unclear manifesto for concerted action. Indeed, at the time of writing, Prime Minister Rishi Sunak had just made a political U-turn on key net zero targets and industrial commitments. It "signal[led] a retrograde step at a time when other countries are accelerating action to decarbonise their economies" said Sarah Ratcliffe, CEO of BBP. And swathes of UK scientists and environmental groups expressed anger: "short-term political gain will undermine the transition to net zero and

3 Guardian, 4 July 2023

with it the future opportunities, prosperity and safety of the entire country."[4].

Nonetheless, there is some light at the edge of this leadership lacuna, and it's not wildfire. On the ground, the socio-economic drivers behind responsible capitalism are greater now than they have ever been. People want change, and despite the best efforts of personal carbon footprint proponents,[5] they can't do it alone. As campaigners, as consumers and ultimately as investors they are looking squarely at corporate colleagues. Relatively nimble and often cross border in reach, businesses certainly have the potential to define and embed global societal change – and Environmental, Social and Governance (ESG) standards are subsequently bedding into the board room, evident also in capital allocations and asset valuations. They are key to the concept of each and every sustainable future, be it environmental, personal or commercial.

The commercial real estate sector in the UK is working hard then to support and promote the necessary net zero transition, despite the policy lacuna. Almost every business needs property to operate and buildings are being developed, redeveloped and operated with a clear eye on carbon emissions. It's simple enough to place the "E" in a property context (see Chapter 3): the physical risks of climate change will pummel bricks and mortar and its services infrastructure whether they are event driven and acute (involving incidents such as floods or cyclones) or the result of chronic, longer-term climactic shifts (such as this year's heat wave). But the "S" picks up on its operational impact on the people in, on and near the buildings; the type of initiatives that directly affect employees, service providers, communities, customers and/or suppliers. The "G" limb is more inward looking, concerned with the organisational structures and processes of the corporates owning and managing property.

4 Professor Dave Reay, executive director of Edinburgh Climate Change Institute, University of Edinburgh, is quoted in Laville, 2023.

5 Solnit, 23 August 2021

Businesses are encouraging the proliferation of industry-set benchmarks, to rate the sustainability of their operations and their property assets. Organisations like the Global Real Estate Sustainability Benchmark (GRESB) generate a rating by considering every aspect of physical, in-building operations, and the extent to which they support broader ESG goals. When it comes to the assets themselves, there is certainly less talk in the property market of a green premium and more of a brown discount, as owners and operators understand that their brand standards are reflected to the outside world in their buildings. Understanding the relationships that play out on land is vital. The well-publicised post-Covid war for talent means the sustainable working environment and clean green air is key to attracting and retaining the best staff. Of vital importance to this book, a new generation of collaborative and innovative landlords and tenants are shifting the dial on traditional practice with green leases.

## Greening the lease

Against this backdrop, green leases offer an exciting opportunity to make a deep, commercially aware and relatively swift sea-change in how the built environment responds to the climate challenge. The companies that fully embrace more impactful green lease drafting can embed in their longstanding commercial relationships and building operations the kind of mitigation measures that could, ultimately, help drive us towards the less terrifying end of that RCP scenario spectrum.

It's early days. There's still no such thing as a market standard, institutionally accepted green lease, but the ideas discussed in Chapter 4 are coalescing around various features that can support the generation and centrality of ESG performance targets in how a building is occupied and operated. Fundamental to their take up then is empowering real estate practitioners and their clients to approach and manipulate them confidently. By first exploring the various tools freely available to help with green lease drafting in Chapter 3, we'll learn how lawyers and industry bodies are devising a new generation of products, of staters for ten on the green lease journey, and see how clients are increasingly keen to understand and adopt these provisions; to learn how their leasing documents can help them meet their own ESG targets, and drive real change.

## Changing the world

To be clear at the outset, greening an investment grade lease is not a straightforward business. Quite apart from the difficulties catering for the nuances of every building; the differing strategic aims of every business; the competitive outputs of every commercial operation; even the differing degrees of every building's reliance on technology or engagement with the local community, the fact is that we are, in the UK's commercial property world, heavily wedded to a model of leasing known as full repairing and insuring (FRI). For decades, FRI principles have underpinned commercial real estate investment. FRI works essentially to push the costs of occupation onto the tenant occupier, thus providing the landlord with a clear (usually) and pleasingly reliable quarterly income stream akin to dividends.

In this well-established FRI world, green leases call for a whole new mind set. To turn sustainable ambition into a lowered emission reality, the parties must work together and commit to shared goals that generally upend FRI concepts. Done properly, both landlord and tenant will now have a stake in the future not only of the square footage itself, but also in its whole environmental lifespan. Rather than signing up to a simple (ish) FRI cash flow mechanism, landlord and tenant must agree to cost sharing, information sharing and ambition sharing with all the gusto that they might have previously lent (and still do lend) to bartering over alienation or user prohibitions.

Added to this conceptual challenge is the fact that the earliest attempts to introduce "green" drafting were both limited and lacklustre. Arguably, this early cul-de-sac of green lease development still taints newer attempts at change; the more visionary landlords' green drafts are regularly redlined by tenant lawyers who are, fairly, used to reading nothing more than a backdoor attempt to shift costs and responsibility onto their clients. Unsurprising then, the early concept has been slow to capture attention and properly bed into the market.

Today though, my experience of the commercial property sector is that many, many companies are serious about the change. Future generations of green leases may have risked starting on the back foot, but they are gaining serious traction. JLL reported in June 2021 that, "globally, 34 percent of occupiers had green lease clauses in 2021, while a further 40 percent plan to sign them by 2025." As the general election lumbers towards us over the horizon, it remains to be seen how any political party will look to formulate and place top-down net zero regulation on the commercial real estate industry, but they would all do well to engage with this forward thinking and surprising nimble sector, to understand what changes are already building the brave new net zero world from the ground up.

# CHAPTER TWO

# BACKGROUND LAW AND REGULATION

> We are lawyers. We work in law firms, or in legal departments in-house. We negotiate clients' transactions, plan for compliance and advise on legal responsibilities. It can be frustrating then that looking for clear and comprehensive framework for green leases is not a particularly fruitful activity. Beyond the ambitious overarching commitments to, and florid column inches on, net zero targets, the UK commercial property market actually has very little by way of detailed direction to go on when It comes to decarbonisation. However, beyond the moveable feast of MEES, any attempt to create a framework is likely to reach out into various legal areas and market practices that traditionally fall well beyond real estate.

Attempts to build a comprehensive legislative and regulatory framework for green leases is necessarily far reaching.

A green lease could include reference to domestic Net Zero targets, but in terms of 'must do's, hands are only really tied by the Minimum Energy Efficiency Standards (MEES)., Thereafter, depending on the scope and ambition of the clauses used, a green lease could pick up on various other elements of law and regulation to deliver on objectives. There is ultimately a potential for constraints within the competition law framework, for example. And overarching this, possibly, is international and EU law (particularly in relation to the potential for cross border data protection law).

Lastly, this Chapter considers the complex menu of national and/or global disclosure requirements for mandatory and voluntary corporate reporting, all set against the proliferation of industry benchmarking tools which provide, when they bite, an interesting backdrop to the motivations of landlords and tenants in adopting green leases.

## 2.1 Nero Zero

### 2.1.1 The introduction of Net Zero targets

As far as the world's major economies are concerned, the Climate Change Act 2008 was a gamechanger, enshrining dramatic emission reduction targets into UK law for the first time. Little more than a decade on, The Climate Change Act 2008 (2050 Target Amendment) Order 2019 (S.I. 2019/1056) then tightened them further. Now, "it is the duty of the Secretary of State to ensure that the net UK carbon account for the year 2050 is at least **100% lower** than the 1990 baseline" (s.1(1)). So the general, national aim is not quite *no* emissions of carbon dioxide and other greenhouse gases then, but it is still an ambitious, evidence-based and independently-assessed reduction – and close enough to be known colloquially as "net zero".

### 2.1.2 So, are we nearly there yet?

By any measure, reaching net zero as a country is a monumental task. To ease the transition, the UK government set an interim legislative target. By 2035, we should aim for a 78% reduction on those 1990 greenhouse gases; a "nearly! three quarters done!" response to perennial "are we nearly there yet?" questions, and a chance to be sure we're on the right track. Similarly, while the devolved administrations (Scotland, Wales and Northern Ireland) are deemed responsible for about a fifth of the UK's emissions, they too picked up the baton and created their own climate change policies to support broader UK-wide goals.[6]

Legally-binding 'carbon budgets' also act as markers on the road to net zero, offering five-yearly caps on greenhouse gas emissions. The exact carbon amounts in these budgets must actually be determined at least 12 years in advance, the idea being that since it will touch on every aspect of the economy, a long lead in time allows businesses and individuals to devise and implement their own plans in response, with a maximum chance of ensuring cost-effectiveness and ultimate success. That said, once set, the Government is also obliged to prepare policies to ensure the success of each carbon budget.

It attempts to do this at every level. It produces a Climate Change Risk Assessment (CCRA) every five years on current *and future* risks to *and opportunities* for the UK from climate change. And this is ultimately informed by the Prime Minister chairing a Cabinet Committee on Climate Change, which filters macro decision-making down through all government departments via various subcommittees so that they are each conscious of climate change in every policy. Two main UK government departments are meanwhile ultimately responsible for action on climate change at home and abroad: the Department for Environment and Rural Affairs (Defra) and the Department for Energy Security and Net Zero (DESNZ).

---

6 In Scotland, The Climate Change (Scotland) Act 2009 commits to a "Net Zero" emissions target of 2045 with periodic target sand a Scottish Climate Change Adaptation Programme. In Wales, The Environment (Wales) Act 2016 placed a duty on Welsh Government to develop carbon budgets for Wales, and aim for a 80% reduction by 2050. In Northern Ireland meanwhile, the Northern Ireland Executive, is developing a new Energy Strategy and seeking advice on how to contribute to UK targets.

### 2.1.3 Scrutiny on progress

Official scrutiny of progress against the net zero target is provided for in the Climate Change Act 2008 itself, with the statutory establishment of an independent Committee on Climate Change (CCC). The remit of the CCC's Adaptation Committee is to advise the UK and devolved governments on climate change risks and assess our government's progress towards tackling and adapting to them. Its annual reports on this are therefore crucial to charting our national progress towards reducing greenhouse gas emissions, and to helping us prepare for and adapt to the impacts of climate change.

In June 2023, the CCC released a damning 437-page progress report to parliament. It concluded that progress against the net zero targets is too slow, and that the UK Government must do more to aid delivery. CCC Chair Lord Debben wrote: "In this report, we comment on a curious situation. This year, the Government has published more detail on their climate programme than ever before, cajoled to do so by the Courts. But Ministers seem less willing to put that programme at the centre of their stated aims. Our confidence in the achievement of the UK's 2030 target [...] has markedly declined from last year.

"The true test of leadership is delivery. And here, I am more worried. The commitment of Government to act has waned since our COP26 Presidency. There is hesitation to commit fully to the key pledges. This will not win the fight. Our successes have come when we have been bold, harnessing the power of the private sector to work collectively towards lower emissions, to the benefit of people across the UK."

### 2.1.4 Net zero delivery for commercial buildings

Thorough consideration of the various targets and assessments of national climate change strategy is, thankfully, beyond the remit of this book, but importantly for the commercial real estate sector, the CCC progress report drew attention to a gaping policy lacuna: "Non-residential buildings need attention. There is a large and increasingly concerning policy gap relating to non-residential buildings. [...] **There are no convincing plans to decarbonise commercial buildings.**"[7] There is simply not enough policy from the UK government to catch up with the science.

This is important. Clearly every sector of the UK economy will need to decarbonise if we are to meet our collective net zero targets, but real estate has one of the highest carbon footprints of any sector. According to the Global Status Report[s] for Buildings and Construction, produced annually by the UN Environmental Programme, it consistently contributes record emission highs. In the UK, the Green Building Council (GBC) has estimated that the UK's built environment contributes about 25% of the country's total GHG emissions (a figure that rises to 42% if elements of surface transport are included).

So not only are we major climate change contributors, we are also sitting ducks for its impacts. When we think about climate related risks, the floods, storms and wildfires in the more extreme RCP scenarios are visceral and terrifying. In the context of the built environment, it is relatively simple to picture physical climate risks causing both direct damage to assets and associated indirect damage, such as to supply, logistics and distribution chain disruption.

But that apocalypse is not quite the whole picture. In June 2017, the Task Force on Climate-related Financial Disclosures (TFCFD) published a Final Report that explained climate-related risks could be divided into two major categories: (1) risks

---

7 See page 141, Chapter 5.

related to the physical impacts of climate change and (2) risks related to the transition to a lower-carbon economy. That second category includes "policy, legal, technology, and market changes to address mitigation and adaptation requirements related to climate change" and it is very real, with an impact that might be both financial and reputational. In more granular detail, understanding this category of risk is key not only to mitigation, but also to identifying opportunities. An organisation might be able to avoid costly and embarrassing litigation, but it might also gain a competitive edge in its market, by investing in innovative green technology.

So then, for all the column inches on net zero, for all the urgent need for action to tackle the climate change crisis and real estate's contributions to and risks from it, clear legislative rules and targets are actually thin on the ground. In fact, the only plain vanilla regulation and government policy in the bricks and mortar of commercial real estate world currently focuses on one thing: the production of Energy Performance Certificates (EPCs) and their use in achieving Minimum Energy Efficiency Standards (MEES).

## 2.2 Energy Performance Certificates (EPCs)

Back in 2007, EPCs[8] were at the heart of the UK Government's response to the EU's Energy Performance of Buildings Directive (EPBD). The certificates must be produced on the occurrence of various transaction triggers involving buildings that are roofed, with walls, and "energy is used to condition the indoor climate". It might therefore relate to a whole or a part of a whole property, depending on how it is structured, but the property must enjoy

---

8 Display Energy Certificates (DECs) are necessary for large buildings (with a total useful floor area over 250m$^2$) that are occupied in whole or part by public authorities and frequently visited by the public.

heating, ventilation and/or air-con, not simply hot water and lighting.

EPCs clearly (arguably crudely) rate a building between A (most efficient) through to G (least efficient). And alongside the given rating, a recommendation report will set out various works that are not mandatory but which could be expected to improve the energy efficiency rating of the asset.

### 2.2.1 When do you need to get an EPC?

Those transaction triggers for the production of an EPC (by a qualified EPC Assessor on behalf of the commissioning owner) are every time a property is:

(i) **Constructed** – when an EPC must be provided on practical completion;

(ii) **Modified** – guidance from the Department for Communities and Local Government suggested in 2017 that this means "a building is modified to have more or fewer parts than it originally had and the modification includes the provision or extension of fixed services for heating, air conditioning or mechanical ventilation";

(iii) **Sold** – an EPC must be commissioned before a property is marketed and provided at the earliest opportunity; or

(iv) **Let** – including in the context of a lease extension, reversionary leases and renewals).

### 2.2.2 Does an EPC have to be registered?

Once on the publicly accessible register (searchable by postcode), an EPC becomes "live" and will last 10 years from its production date. After this, it lapses with no automatic requirement to renew. Before it is registered, the EPC is "draft" and can, in the commercial world at least, have been commissioned as an information gathering exercise for a number of different reasons, including for example planning for MEES compliance or capital expenditure.

### 2.2.3 Are there any exemptions?

Very few buildings are fundamentally exempt from the requirement for an EPC, however these include buildings which are:

- **'small'** – where detached with a useful floor area less than $50m^2$;
- **due to be demolished** – provided planning and conservation consents have been obtained, and the resulting site would be suitable for redevelopment;
- **listed or officially protected**[9] – where the minimum energy performance requirements would unacceptably alter it;

---

9 It's worth a note here to stress that of course listed buildings (those on a statutory list of Buildings of Special Architectural or Historic Interest) are not fundamentally excluded from the EPC (or MEES) regulations. In practice, any recommended improvement will need to be assessed in context. As DCLG explained: "You might not need an EPC. What matters is where EPC report recommendations "would unacceptably alter their character or appearance". EPC recommendations might involve installing double glazing or external wall insulation, for example, and this

- **temporary** – meaning it is only going to be used for 2 years or less;
- **places of worship** – or used for other religious activities; or
- **low energy demand** – industrial sites, workshops and non-residential agricultural buildings with low energy demand which accommodate industrial activities in spaces without air conditioning.

### 2.2.3 What was the impact of EPCs?

It's fair to point out that, from a legal point of view, the early years of EPC production were uneventful. The rating offered by an EPC was not all that impactful on the completion of a transaction. The technology for a desktop survey was rudimentary and, while some buyers or tenants made the practical linkage between an inefficient building and higher running costs, the full extent of MEES had yet to bite.

For completeness, arguing that the party entitled to the EPC wasn't interested in receiving it was (and is) no defence to failing to produce a certificate when required. Still, the penalties were

---

would "result in unacceptable alterations in the majority of historic buildings". If the recommendation report suggests anything too intrusive or structural then, the property could be exempt from the need for an EPC. On the other hand, recommendations to install new bulbs or loft insulation might not be problematic. DCLG concluded that building owners will need to take a view. In practice, this is likely to mean obtaining *draft* EPCs, reading the recommendations and considering each listed building on a case-by-case basis. Do remember however that listings rarely protect *whole* buildings, and if the recommendations *could* be carried out without unacceptably altering character or appearance, an EPC might be required but so too, possibly, is listed building consent. See paragraph 2.3.2 for the potential to rely on a third-party consent exemption to MEES if this is not forthcoming.

(and are) not dramatic. The resultant fine is calculated by a formula using 12.5% of the rateable value of the building, and subject to a maximum of £5,000 (Regulation 38, The Energy Performance of Buildings (England and Wales) Regulations 2012). Failing to produce an EPC could admittedly complicate obtaining building regulations compliance certification on a construction or modification project but, generally speaking, there were no legislative consequences to receiving notification of a poor rating. Simply owning or letting a property with a poor rating was not unlawful. Then MEES arrived.

## 2.3 Minimum Energy Efficiency Standards (MEES)

Emerging originally from the Energy Act 2011, The Energy Efficiency (Private Rented Property) (England and Wales) Regulations 2015 (MEES) were drafted by the Department for Business, Energy & Industrial Strategy (BEIS), and they originally navigated with official associated guidance provided by BEIS and the Department for Communities and Local Government. Interestingly, MEES were a UK-only initiative, linked to the Government's Clean Growth Strategy, and the power of their application is in the sideways pressure they apply on landlords when it comes to ensuring commercial stock is energy efficient.

Remember there is no positive statutory requirement to carry out energy improvement recommendations, but MEES applies pressure on landlords in other ways. Regulation 27 effectively controls the efficiency standards of buildings by limiting how they can be let. Property owners or landlords could not:

- from 1 April 2018 – grant a new tenancy or an extension or renewal of an existing tenancy of substandard property; or

- from 1 April 2023 – *continue* to let substandard property on such a tenancy.

### 2.3.1 What are the penalties for breaching MEES?

At its inception, the impact of MEES was expected to be dramatic, with estimates from BEIS that 18% of commercial buildings in the country were failing to meet the E rating standard.[10] According to Legal Futures there are still at the time of writing over 19,000 commercial properties with sub-standard ratings.

The financial penalties which can be imposed by the Local Authority/Local Weights and Measures Authorities (LWMAs) for a breach can be severe. Under regulation 41, these are set by reference to the property's rateable value and the length of time of non-compliance. If this is less than three months, it is the greater of £5,000 or 10% RV (to a maximum of £50,000). For more than 3 months in breach, the penalty becomes the greater of £10,000 or 20% RV (to a maximum of £150,000). While the enforcement authority should not impose a financial penalty twice in relation to the same breach of MEES, it is easy to see how the sums could add up in a multi-tenanted building.

MEES also has in its arsenal a "publication penalty" (regulation 39), which threatens to name and shame the landlords guilty of non-compliance on the PRS Exemptions Register. And importantly, in the context of available penalties, it is important to note that just because a lease was granted (or exists) in contravention of MEES, it does not, legally, determine. In default of MEES, the offending lease remains valid and

10 BEIS, 2014, p. 89.

enforceable as between the landlord and the tenant (regulation 30).

Interestingly however, over five years after the introduction of MEES, the impact of any enforcement has yet to be felt. For a long time, resourcing was blamed. Local enforcement teams were simply not incentivised to collect fines on behalf of the central government pot. The Housing and Planning Act 2016 changed that, giving Local Authorities the ability to keep civil penalties such as those generated by MEES. Practical problems still remain in terms of identifying non-compliant properties, capacity building for enforcement teams and incentivising tenants to complain. Nonetheless, landlords should not expect the status quo to continue.

### 2.3.2 When does MEES not apply?

To avoid stumbling into the MEES trap, building owners need to be certain that they are either fundamentally exempt from the regime; clear that they are granting a lease which is not prohibited by the regulation; or confident that they will be able to register an exemption, which can protect them from compliance for a limited period of time.

*Are you fundamentally excluded?*

With the effluxion of time, this category is always shrinking, but remember that MEES simply does not apply on buildings without an EPC, either because the building was *not required* to have an EPC in the first place, or because a transactional trigger has not occurred. As time passes the likelihood of encountering this situation is reduced, but of course a lease could be continuing although it was granted before the EPC regulations were introduced.

*Are you granting a lease which is not prohibited?*

Regulation 23(3)) is clear that a landlord can grant a lease over (or continue to let) substandard properties on tenancies that are granted for a term of:

(i) over 99 years; or

(ii) less than six months (provided there hasn't already been continuous occupation for 12 months and there is no right of renewal or extension).

*Are you able to claim an exemption?*

Every exemption is personal to the building owner (i.e. non transferrable to a new owner) and they must be registered *before the letting is made,* or *continued to be let after 1 April 2023,* on the PRS Exemptions Register. Registration itself can be an administrative chore, but every exemption (except where detailed below) is valid for five years. Thereafter, a landlord must either comply with MEES or again demonstrate another exemption. There is a clear emphasis on proactively understanding and managing the client's approach to MEES compliance.

The exemptions for compliance in commercial property are listed in the regulations:

- **Devaluation (regulations 32(1) and 36 (2))** – if an independent surveyor on the Royal Institution of Chartered Surveyors (RICS) register of valuers determines that the market value is likely to be reduced by more than 5%, as a result of the relevant improvements.

- **Structural damage (regulation 28(2))** – if the recommended improvement puts the property at risk.

- **Cost-effectiveness ("7-year payback rule") (regulation 28(3))** – if an independent energy assessor determines that the cost of purchasing and installing potential improvements would not pay for themselves through energy savings within seven years.

- **'All Improvements Made' (regulation 25)** – where all the "relevant energy efficiency improvements" have been made (or none can be made) and the property remains sub-standard.

- **Third party consent (regulation 31)** – if, having used reasonable efforts to obtain it, a tenant, a head landlord, mortgagee or the planning authorities refuse consent for works or apply conditions the landlord cannot reasonably comply with. This exemption lasts five years or earlier, if the situation changes).

- **Wall insulation (regulation 24(2))** – some wall insulation systems may not be suitable in certain situations due to a potential negative impact on the fabric or structure of the property.

- **'New Landlord' Exemption (regulations 33(1) and 36 (2))** – this (even more) temporary six month exemption applies in some limited circumstances where it would be inappropriate or unreasonable for a landlord to be required to comply with MEES immediately. This includes:

  (A) the purchase of an investment interest in a let property;

  (B) a new lease granted under the 1954 Act or a contingent agreement for lease; and

(C) tenant insolvency (should its guarantor become a landlord in taking over the lease).

### 2.3.3 What is, and what may be, a substandard property?

At the time of writing, "substandard" properties are those with an EPC rating of F or G, but it is important to be aware that there is broad expectation that this concept of substandard is *probably* on a dramatic upwards trajectory.

Early in 2021, BEIS launched two new major consultations on building energy performance. Each of these documents set out a step change in action on energy efficiency for buildings, aimed at helping to meet the UK's net zero target.

The first, "Non-domestic Private Rented Sector minimum energy efficiency standards: EPC B implementation" (the "**EPC B Consultation**"), set out an ambitious future trajectory for MEES with the implementation of a minimum B standard by 2030 (where cost effective). The proposed timeline for the implementation of this new standard included a series of compliance windows:

- by and from 1 April 2025: All landlords have to present a valid EPC;
- by and from 1 April 2027: MEES to stipulate a minimum EPC C standard; and then
- by and from 1 April 2030: MEES to stipulate a minimum EPC B standard.

Importantly, the EPC B Consultation heralded a move away from enforcement at the point of letting. With *all* landlords required to present valid EPCs in 2025, the need to demonstrate MEES compliance (or register a valid exemption) would become a constant ongoing requirement and not one triggered by the grant of a lease.

The EPC B Consultation also detailed various Improvements to the application and enforcement of MEES, including (inter alia):

- a new six-month temporary exemption to MEES compliance for shell and core properties;

- a new property compliance and exemptions database, to be operated by a third party and requiring payment of an undetermined registration fee per property;

- new penalties for landlords who fail to register on that proposed database or provide a valid EPC when required. As an aside, if it becomes possible for penalty fines for any particular breach to be applied on more than one occasion, this will be a real concern given the potential for a continual breach since 1 April 2023;

- the introduction of a standardised 'payback calculator', to assist parties seeking to take advantage of the cost effectiveness exemption to MEES compliance (see paragraph 2.3.2 and Regulation 28(3)), by helping in the calculation of purchase and installation costs of the relevant energy efficiency improvement; and

- a tightened requirement to provide a valid EPC prior to marketing a property, essentially prohibiting selling agents from advertising and letting properties unless they are able to provide an EPC.

Promisingly, it was acknowledged that greater clarity in respect of EPC and MEES obligations is required for listed, conservation area and mixed-use buildings, and the government recognised the need to split responsibility for compliance more clearly between landlord and tenant (including with duties of cooperation for both), but there is not much detail in the EPC B Consultation on how exactly this will be done.

*When could the law change?*

This EPC B Consultation closed on 9 June 2021 and in its immediate aftermath, legislation was anticipated to be in force from April 2025. Since that date however, for two and a half years (at the time of writing), the gov.uk consultation website has been static: "We are analysing your feedback. Visit this page again soon to download the outcome to this public feedback."

In fairness, while the change failed to find itself on the statue books, it was pursued by a number of politicians. The Minimum Energy Performance of Buildings (No. 2) Bill (Bill 150 2021-22) was a private member's bill was introduced into the House of Lords by the Liberal Democrat peer Lord Foster of Bath, and the Conservative Sir Roger Gale in the House of Commons, on 20 July 2021. It deals briefly (efficiently) with the application of MEES to commercial real estate and the subject matter of the EPC B Consultation:

> "*7 Rented non-domestic buildings*
>
> *(1) All rented non-domestic buildings must be EPC Band B by 2030, subject to the exemptions under subsection (2).*
>
> *(2) The exemptions referred to in subsection (1) are—*
>
> *a. where it is not technically feasible, and*
>
> *b. where it is not cost-effective as defined under section 1(4), to achieve EPC Band B,*

*in which case such properties must be improved to an EPC level to which these exemptions do not apply.*

(3) *The Secretary of State may, by notice in writing, direct any relevant person to comply with this section.*

(4) *The Secretary of State may make regulations for the purpose of ensuring compliance with this section."*

The drafting is clear enough, albeit brief compared to the ambition of the EPC B Consultation, but the Bill seems to have stalled. Parliament UK is clear that this type of private member's bill (a Presentation Bill), which is formally introduced by members who do not speak in support of it, "rarely become law". Still, the parliamentary debate reports in Hansard reveal that the second reading, at which more detailed debate may be expected, was once expected to take place on 24 November this year. Whether or not this takes place remains to be seen.

Many in the market are entirely unconvinced that law resulting from this EPC B Consultation can possibly be brought to bear in the time scales it anticipated. At this stage, even assuming political will, a simple debate path and critical timetabling, royal assent for the Bill is unlikely until late 2024 at the earliest. And in the meantime, in September 2023, Prime Minister Rishi Sunak dramatically pivoted on a similar trajectory for residential MEES requirements, scrapping changes that would have made it unlawful for new leases of homes to have an EPC rating of C by 2025 (and all leases to meet that new standard by 2028).

In fact, the Government was notably silent on plans for *commercial* MEES, however building owners and occupiers would arguably be wise to look to continue with any plans to increase the energy efficiency of their assets by the end of the decade. In some cases capital expenditure plans have already been formulated and money has been spent. Tenants are certainly keeping a close eye, given that the weight of energy costs in inefficient buildings will almost certainly fall on their balance sheets[11] . Ultimately, divergent categories of standard real estate could see different capital and rental valuations.

Also, of course, Sunak's U-turn was in anticipation of a general election in 2024 that is likely to see the political parties split on how the financial burden and inconvenience of climate policies falls on voters[12]. MEES, for example, emerged under the then Liberal Democrat Energy & Climate Change Secretary Ed Davy, who is now party leader and remains reportedly committed to climate change action. Labour has vowed to "stand firm on net zero policies". The current Government may be focused on neutralising political rebellion from within its supporter base, but assuming a different future government believes in the impetus for hiking commercial MEES standards, it is important not to be caught out.

## 2.4 The introduction of a new property rating system

The second BEIS consultation from back in early 2021 related to a suggestion that a new sector specific performance-based ratings (PBR) system could be introduced: "Introducing a Performance-Based Policy Framework in large Commercial and Industrial Buildings in England and Wales" (the "**PBR Consultation**").

The ultimate impact of any regulation in this area is an unknown, but the PRS Consultation speaks directly to the growing appreciation that there is little correlation between an EPC rating and a building's actual in-use energy/carbon performance – you

11 Analysis in the residential context claimed that delaying a minimum EPC C rating under MEES to 2030 would add £1.4bn to the cost of energy bills, assuming a medium gas price scenario. Smeeton, 2023.

12 Pickard et al, 20 September 2023.

can install all the loft insulation in the world, but still operate with the heating cranked up and the windows open.

It remains unclear what exactly a new operating rating would cover (such as water use). Also, no exemptions are proposed to this new system save for reasons related to national security, and BEIS indicated that it is still considering how breaches of PRS requirements (e.g. failure to onboard a property or submit data) would be enforced.

Still, the idea broadly was that a new PBR scheme would apply first in 2022/23 to commercial offices above 1,000m$^2$ (with different sectors then coming onboard across the next decade). Obligated owners of buildings or single occupational tenants (it is not yet clear precisely which party would be responsible where there is a more complex holding structure) would be required to 'on board' their building into a new framework. This would involve assessment by a qualified person to gather relevant information (such as the address, floor space, operational hours, use, energy meters set up, etc). Thereafter, annual energy use data should be submitted annually, with the idea that the building can be given an energy intensity rating on a 'per m2 ' basis. This rating will be publicly available inside the building and online.

The proposed PBR scheme is broadly modelled on an Australian equivalent, the National Australian Built Environment Rating System (NABERS), which has been successfully benchmarking the operational efficiency of buildings in Australia since Kylie was releasing her second studio album in 1989. A national initiative managed by the NSW Government on behalf of the Federal, State and Territory governments of Australia, NABERS effectively provides a comparable sustainability measurement. Using the principle that "What gets measured gets managed," buildings (including hotels, shopping centres, apartments, offices, and data centres), are awarded between one and six stars for energy, water, waste and indoor environment. The ratings last

12 months and offer a simple framework for annual reporting and sustainability strategies. The organization reports on its website that its customers consequently save "an average of 30-40% on their energy over 10 years", a statistic that can drive financial growth and portfolio returns.

NABERS was actually launched in the UK in November 2020, and run until recently by the Building Research Establishment (BRE) as scheme administrator. An overseeing steering committee comprises BRE, the Better Buildings Partnership and NABERS, and there are currently two product offerings for UK office buildings, with ratings carried out by UK-trained assessors:

- Design for Performance to drive energy efficient new buildings (https://files.bregroup.com/nabers/NABERS_UK_DfP_Fact_Sheet.pdf), and

- NABERS UK Energy for Offices ratings (NABERS UK – Energy for Offices – BRE Group).

As for the EPC B Consultation, the gov.uk website reveals only that the Government is still "analysing your feedback". It remains to be seen then whether a new (additional) performance-based scheme could indeed make it far simpler to rate and benchmark a property's energy use, ultimately changing behaviour and supporting the transition to a low carbon economy. Would new regulations complement or replace MEES? Perhaps a new PBR scheme would just introduce unnecessary complexity in an already blurry landscape. Landlord ratings will be affected by tenant activity, for example, so will leases impose greater responsibility on tenant behaviour? BEIS reportedly prefers a hybrid approach for the two systems, whereby landlords will remain subject to MEES compliance and need to present a valid EPC at 'onboarding'.

Either way, the chances of any new PBR scheme being implemented wholesale within the timeframes envisaged by the PBR Consultation are fast evaporating. Additionally, both the MEES trajectory and the new PBR are going to involve some serious investment at an asset and an industry level and in this context green leases are a fascinating industry-led solution to some of the problems while the commercial real estate sector waits for actual policy to emerge from the gloom.

## 2.5 Other areas of law and regulation

Outside the regulation, such as it exists, for the built environment, there are other areas of law that can impact on green lease drafting. Without intending to be comprehensive, it is possible, for example, that:

### 2.5.1 Competition law

Interestingly, there has been some concern that the environmental and sustainability agreements and corporate co-operation strategies routinely envisioned by green leases (see Chapter 4, paragraph 4.1) *may* be captured by the prohibitions of competition law.

The problem is in Chapter 1, section 2 of the Competition Act 1998 (CA 1998). This section prohibits agreements and practices between horizontal entities which have "as their object or effect the prevention, restriction, or distortion of competition". Clearly many agreements in a letting context are de facto untroubled by this (as landlords and tenants are not competing in the same industry), but arguably competitive tenants on an estate could fall foul of the strict rules.

There was some initial relief in section 9 of the CA 1998, which offers a broad exemption where those agreements "contribute to improving the production or distribution… or to promoting technical progress, while allowing consumers a fair share of the resulting benefit" (provided they do not actually eliminate or distort competition to an appreciable extent). Applying this exemption has been complex however in an environmental agreement context, especially given its third limb (consumer benefit). "In-market" efficiencies, the traditional kind that counts for the competition authorities, could only benefit that narrow group who actually buy a product, so proponents of environmental strategies and agreements are now actually looking at "out of market" benefits for an impact on broader society.

Amid growing pressure, the UK's Competition and Markets Authority (CMA) published Green Agreements Guidance in October 2023 on environmental sustainability agreements, setting out a more flexible approach to enforcing competition law when it comes to "legitimate environmental initiatives". Understanding and evidencing, whether any particular agreement will qualify as legitimate is not always an exact science. It's a balancing act.

It would seem possible for example that any agreement that ultimately restricts the use or development of more environmentally sustainable products or services, or is found to limit quality or innovation, could be a problem for the CMA. Landlords and tenants might make the most of the CMA's unusual offer of an "open door" policy to get informal guidance up front where the balancing act is not clear.

### 2.5.2 Greenwashing and greenhushing

The topic of greenwashing, and greenhushing, is considered further in Chapter 3, paragraph 3.3.1, in the context of its being a legal risk to how green initiatives such as green lease drafting and commitments may be received, is discussed at that point;

### 2.5.3 Data protection law

Data protection is a clear example of international law that can bite on green lease provisions within and without our territorial borders. Data (whether mandating, collecting, storing and/or analysing it) is necessarily at the root of any successful sustainable strategy. *You can't manage what you don't measure.* And as the proptech industry gathers serious stream, so too does the proliferation of products that are designed to collect and harness data relating to a building's use and occupation.

This book considers broad drafting for ESG data collection and use in both Chapter 3 paragraph 3.3.3 and Chapter 4 paragraph 4.3 but, before we get that far, it is worth understanding a very basic context of the UK's data protection regime.

Depending on the scope of the corporate activities and the extent to which data may be exported, UK companies may be captured by various different rules. Those incorporated and operating solely within our territorial borders however will likely be captured at least by the Data Protection Act 2018, which implemented the General Data Protection Regulation ((EU) 2016/679) in this jurisdiction following Brexit (UK GDPR).

The UK GDPR restricts the processing of personal data by most public and private data controllers, while appreciating that personal data knows no borders and yet ultimately underpins and supports trade and business. In the real estate world, a UK private sector entity looking lawfully to disclose and/or process personal data on a systematic and routine basis should remember that breach could result in statutory sanctions as well as contractual liability and reputational damage. It makes sense then at the outset of any data sharing arrangement to analysis properly how and to what extent the proposed activity needs to comply. Which party is in fact the controller (who determines the purposes and means of the processing of personal data, under

Article 4(7), UK GDPR), and/or which the processor (who processes personal data on behalf of a controller and acts on its instructions, as per Article 28(3), UK GDPR), for example? Obligations in the UK GDPR can range from the need for anonymisation and pseudonymisation to certain technical and security requirements, to even carrying out a data protection impact assessment (DPIA).

## 2.6 Disclosure and reporting standards

There's no doubt that the intersection of investor pressure and forthcoming regulation is already a fertile ground for the creation of comprehensive, high-quality and auditable climate disclosure. This, according to research by the Urban Land Institute, is already starting to "reshape traditional investment decision-making processes".[13] And it is also inevitably leading to burgeoning interest in green leases. As the real estate industry reports transparently on climate risks that affect its operations, so too will it have to plan to adapt to those climate impacts, and draft contracts that support decarbonisation.

For completeness, then it is worth noting that many companies have been voluntarily reporting on ESG metrics for several years already, however regulation in this space is, and will be, undoubtedly increasing. With both the Bank of England and the Financial Conduct Authority (FCA) ranking physical and transition climate risk as a significant threat to the economy, regulatory change is certain. Until reporting requirements are completely standardised however, it is often at the discretion of individual companies to implement their own reporting plans and respond to investor pressure regarding climate-related data.

13 Haggerty, 2023.

### 2.6.1 The rationale for reporting and reporting standards

The World Economic Forum has long been very clear that increased reporting of sustainability metrics will drive corporate transformations in:

- **Organisation** – as firms identify internal gaps and address sustainability as a strategic issue;
- **Culture** – with closer collaboration and engagement between parts of a business;
- **Digitisation** – as companies start to prioritise and leverage data; and
- **Brand** – with companies building narratives around ESG commitments and values.

### 2.6.2 Understanding the extant reporting frameworks

Appreciating the differences between the structures and timelines of the available frameworks, both mandatory and voluntary, both in force and proposed, is important, particularly where data requirements in green leases are designed to service reporting obligations.

Broadly speaking, in the UK, the frameworks currently include various ways to make both GHG emissions and climate risks transparent. There is also a distinction to be made between those frameworks which embed the concept of 'double materiality' (recognising both the risks that the climate has on an organisation and the impact an organisation has on a climate), in contrast to those which are centred mainly on the impact of climate risk on the organisation:

### 2.6.2.1 Task Force on Climate-Related Financial Disclosures (TCFD)

TCFD based reporting has in recent years become the 'gold standard' for climate-related disclosures[14] and will ultimately be mandated in the UK for financial institutions (including banks, building societies and insurers), listed companies, asset managers and asset owners; more than 1,300 of the largest UK-registered companies and financial institutions. The TCFD regime consists of 11 recommended disclosures relating to governance, strategy, risk management, and metrics and targets. Interestingly, it is not built around double materiality, but it does contain requirements for the reporting of Scope 1, 2 and 3 emissions (see Chapter 6, paragraph 3.3).

### 2.6.2.2 The International Sustainability Standards Board (ISSB)

The ISSB released draft standards last year for climate and sustainability related disclosures, in line with TCFD recommendations. These were finalised in June 2023 and will be effective from 1 January 2024, at which time the monitoring responsibilities of the TCFD will be transferred to the ISSB. The ISSB standards were hailed by ISSB Chair, Emmanuel Faber, as providing "further clarification of the so-called 'alphabet soup' of ESG initiatives for companies and investors."[15]

The new standards are expected to be adopted under UK law by July 2024 in the form of the UK Sustainability Disclosure Standards.[16] The FCA expects to consult in the first half of 2024 on updating its TCFD-aligned disclosure rules for listed

14 According to the most recent status report of the TCFD, there are now over 4,850 supporters of TCFD around the world.

15 IFRS, 10 July 2023

16 https://www.gov.uk/guidance/uk-sustainability-disclosure-standards

companies to refer to the new standards, with the new requirements expected to be in force from 2025.

### 2.6.2.3 The Financial Conduct Authority's (FCA)'s Sustainability Disclosure Requirements and Investment Labels regime

This FCA consultation paper dated 25 October 2022 proposes sustainability disclosure requirements, a product labelling regime that will "help consumers navigate the market for sustainable investment products" and an 'anti-greenwashing' rule. Following a significant response to that consultation, final rules are expected by the end of 2023.

Where a company's operations reach further afield, other reporting requirements could well bite. Of these, possibly the most relevant are:

- in the US, the Securities and Exchange Commission (SEC) has proposed mandatory climate reporting for issuers and certain investment advisers and investment companies. Clearly there are a variety of political hoops for the SEC to navigate but, if enacted, it could require much of the real estate industry around the world to increase its data disclosure on climate risk and emissions; and

- in the EU, **The Sustainable Finance Disclosure Regulation (SFDR) 2019**[17][1]. The SFDR indeed provides a useful example of how, with sufficient and consistent political will (in this case its 2018 Sustainable Finance Action Plan and its 2019 European Green Deal), the EU became a forerunner in the development of a

[17] Early birds as regards corporate sustainability reporting were the Regulation (EU) No 537/2014, Directive 2004/109/EC, Directive 2006/43/EC and Directive 2013/34/EU.

sustainability-related disclosure regime[18]. Where it applies, the SFDR requires asset managers and other financial market participants to disclose and report on their sustainable investments, at an entity and product level.[19] Large companies must now also comply with detailed reporting requirements in the Corporate Sustainability Reporting Directive (CSRD)[20], and the European Sustainable Reporting Standards (ESRS) will soon pick up on every ESG angle. Operationally, this reporting is supported by the EU's developing Taxonomy Regulation, which uses classification to determine if an economic activity is sustainable and factors in the whole life cycle of a building, including its construction, modification and operation.[21]

## 2.7 The role of investment benchmarks

On a similar note, leaving aside mandatory and voluntary reporting requirements, the real estate industry has for the past couple of decades prioritised its own solutions to assessing a

18 Although this comes with the caveat that while the SFDR has a number of positive elements, it is not necessarily being used in the way it was designed. It was intended to be about transparency but has been used more as a labelling scheme. There have also been a number of challenges in interpreting the provisions of SFDR. It is too early to say whether a SFDR 2.0 is on its way, but the EU Commission launched two consultations in September 2023 that focus on how the SFDR is working in practice and issues in its implementation.

19 Regulation (EU) 2019/2088 of the European Parliament and of the Council of 27 November 2019.

20 Directive (EU) 2022/2464 of the European Parliament and of the Council of 14 December 2022

21 Regulation (EU) 2020/852 of the European Parliament and of the Council of 18 June 2020.

building's operational performance when it comes to energy use and sustainability. A fragmented ratings industry now exists for benchmarking investments, and while the key players can be expected ultimately to consolidate, there are useful considerations when it comes to the contents of a green lease. These are explored in Chapter 3, paragraph 3.4.7 in relation to the determination of a GRESB rating, by way of a benchmarking example.

# CHAPTER THREE

# THE NEW GENERATION OF GREEN LEASES

We have explored the absence of a clear and comprehensive legislative or policy direction, but also set the scene for how a new generation of green lease drafting is, gradually, stepping to that breach.

The market is prioritising its own solutions to the climate crisis, an attempt to fill the gaps left by minimal regulation. Clients are increasingly keen to understand and adopt standards across their businesses and working relationships, not least where they touch on land. And driven by industry bodies and key market players, facilitated by real estate lawyers, green lease provisions can effectively be seen as the glue that holds these initiatives together across sectors, interests and even jurisdictions.

When it comes to incorporating green leases into your professional arsenal, this chapter will first explore a little deeper into the client-specific rationale for considering the drafting, and then run through the various tools and toolkits that have been professionally created and are freely available to help with drafting.

## 3.1 Setting the scene for green leasing

### 3.1.1 Finding and setting a market standard

In any scenario, the exact contents of a green lease clause is clearly going to differ depending on a variety of moveable features. These will include:

- **particular features of the subject building** – For example: is its EPC rating high, or does it need considerable investment? What technology is already collecting relevant data?

- **asset credentials or history** – in terms of valuing square footage at the higher end of the market, environmental credentials are routinely credited as being a differentiator, so there is something to protect against older, more inefficient space.

- **the priorities of the relevant asset class or sector** – beyond an immediate property footprint, tensions clearly exist in certain sectors. Perhaps the industry is very public facing and therefore more visible, and accountable, to a broader audience than 'just' the parties' shareholders and investors. Perhaps, as in life science labs or data centres, processing equipment dictates a larger than average energy draw, necessarily affecting the realistic aims of any green targets.

- **whether the property is standalone or estate-based** – landlords with properties situated on a campus development or retail or industrial park, for example, will likely be keener to ensure standardisation across the tenancies on site.

- **parties' negotiating power** – that old letting chestnut is truer than ever when it comes to incorporating new clauses, especially those with cost consequences. Tenants who bring a good covenant to the negotiating table can tend to leave it with more.

- **client appetite/goal** – it's hard to overestimate the power of this as a driver for green leasing. Perhaps your client is anxious to meet certain reporting standards, or attract a new generation of workforce talent focused on the environmental quality of its workplace. When it comes to exploring client appetite, the questions in paragraph 3.1.2 can be helpful.

As yet then, it's no surprise there is no market standard form of "green lease", but that's not to say that ideas aren't certainly coalescing around the utility of particular clauses to import green ideas, or to address particular ESG challenges.

### 3.1.2 What even is ESG in a leasing environment?

Identifying necessary ESG measures to incorporate into lease agreements and aligning them with key stakeholders' concerns for example is a complex exercise.

Attempts to capture what exactly the notion of ESG could possibly mean in any given sector are fraught with difficulty. There's no categoric or extensive definition ready for application to any particular industry. It's also necessarily personal to every individual corporation in each individual transaction, in each individual asset.

It's probably easier then to set out a workflow framework that can be used by companies and practitioners to tease out a relevant definition of ESG in any given circumstance. In May 2023, the Amsterdam-based Urban Land Institute set out a series of self-assessment questions to enable real estate managers and operators to start to shape their ESG ambitions. These questions include:

- In which jurisdiction do you operate? Where are your assets and where are your (target) investors?
- Which regulation applies in those countries/regions?

- What stakeholders (type, geographic domicile, etc) do you have and what are their ESG-specific requirements?

- What is your level of ambition? Do you want to implement only the minimum market requirements? Do you want to set priorities that go beyond the minimum requirements? Do you want to become a strategic leader in ESG in the real estate sector?"

- Do you have specific building level targets?

With answers to questions like these, real estate players can start to articulate how the rigours of ESG factors will shape their operations, and their contractual relationships. It will start to help define what corporate success will look like, within the need to "promote the success of the company" (as required by section 172 of the Companies Act 2006), and drafting success will look like for any resultant green lease.

## 3.2 Articulating the advantages of Green Leases

### 3.2.1 Acting for landlords

Aside from macro motivations around longer-term climate change mitigation and sustainability, landlords and property owners might well consider that embracing green leasing at their properties will help them today. In particular, green lease drafting can:

1. *Anticipate and deal with transition risks* – transition risks are that category of climate risks discussed in Chapter 2, paragraph 2.1.4, things that arise as a result of the social and economic transition to a lower carbon economy.

2. *Increased corporate and asset marketability* – by addressing sustainability demands from investors/tenants, the landlord is appealing to two vital markets, protecting and securing the value of its own capitalisation as well as its assets (from both a capital and rental point of view). The concept of green leases is certainly bedding-in from a capital allocation perspective, as the commercial property investment market starts to assess the sustainability of assets less from a perspective of a green premium, and more from a need to factor in the risks of brown obsolescence.

3. *Improve market reputation and protect net zero/ESG commitments* – many real estate companies are well-versed in reporting/reducing the impacts of their *own* operations, but they also need to consider emissions arising through their value chains and supply agreements with third parties (Scope 3 emissions, as discussed further in Chapter 6, paragraph 6.2.1). This includes tenants.

4. *Deal with regulatory concerns* – every landlord will be concerned to comply with environmental regulation where it applies and future-proof its asset for upcoming regulation, for example the likely MEES trajectory (see Chapter 2, paragraph 2.3.3)

5. *Build a comprehensive data repository* – and this data is potentially useful for operational decisions as well as sustainability and ESG reporting and disclosure requirements (see Chapter 2, paragraph 2.6).

6. *Improve cash flow and avoid capex shocks* – drafting can enable landlords and asset owners to reduce the risks of capex shocks inherent in any manifestation of physical or transition risks (for example ameliorating not just the costs of remedying flood damage but also easing asset insurance

premiums, allowing expenditure to be spread more equally).

7. *Respond to tenant demands* – last but by no means least, the chance at the heart of green leases to align business interests with the tenant is a compelling one. It can drive "stickiness" and encourage long term, and mutually beneficial relationships and commitments to property assets.

### 3.2.2 Acting for tenants

Tenants are clearly not asset *owners*, and cannot be expected to be overly concerned by the inherent value and marketability of a property for a day longer than the length of their lease interest. It's unsurprising then that for many, concern over the cost consequences of environmental or sustainability initiatives, and an abiding suspicion that it is being relied upon to pay the landlord's bill for longer term asset improvement, drives some reluctance towards green lease drafting. Further consideration of the cultural problems facing parties born and bred in an FRI context is made in paragraph 3.32.

Nonetheless, signing a green lease where or when it is offered can offer potentially significant benefits for a tenant, above the operational security of possession:

1. *Operational cost-savings* – first and foremost, Landlords will likely point in negotiations to the likelihood that increased energy efficiency, the driver behind many green leases clauses, is likely to lead to lower running costs and potential cost savings for the tenant when it comes to its utility bills.

2. *Delivery of organisational net zero/ESG commitments* – The size, sector and brand values of the tenant, as well as its own board level commitments to ESG targets, will clearly

determine how amenable it is likely to be during green lease negotiations. Many tenants will be keen to ensure their own internal ESG policies can be delivered, and will be happy to bring the lease on board as a tool for that task. Reporting requirements (such as discussed in Chapter 2. paragraph 2.6) can also drive engagement, and ensure a tenant is fully engaged in a landlord's measurable, implementable plan for sustainability.

3. *Enhancing the working environment for employees* – business tenants will have an eye firmly on attracting and retaining a workforce by demonstrating sustainable values. This is perhaps more important in some sectors than others, but generally in the well-discussed, post-Covid war for talent, and the reported reluctance to return-to-the-office, any opportunity to enhance the employee experience with "greener" environments is welcome. The result, in the office sector, is a call for flexibility and a rejection of homogeneity. As the IMT predicts (see paragraph 3.4.6 for more on IMT): "By 2030, [ESG] investing frameworks will evolve to effectively value the quality of employment that companies provide [which] will mean that real estate [...] will be as diverse as the American population."

### 3.2.3 Acting for funders

The commercial real estate market in the UK is highly reliant on debt financing. Be aware then that a funder's due diligence on purchase or development (or similarly the act of producing a prospectus for investors) is increasingly concerned with the contents of documents such as sustainability reports and green leases. As well as using funding commitments to evidence its own ESG targets, a funder will of course be assessing the secured asset from the point of view of a potential step-in. If the loan defaults, what kind of asset will the funder take over?

This concern is arguably a relatively new development. Historically, lenders have not, for example, *needed* to consider EPCs. A debt funding is not a trigger event under the EPC regulations (discussed in Chapter 2, paragraph 2.2.1) so need not even be produced. Nonetheless, in practice by far the majority of lenders (like buyers on a corporate purchase, who are also not technically triggering mandatory EPC production) will now ask to see an EPC as part of their due diligence. Clearly, lenders need now to be confident in the secured asset's general regulatory compliance under MEES. Were leases in place at secured assets granted in compliance with MEES?

Interestingly there *could* be other changes afoot to MEES that are *specifically* relevant to funders. The Minimum Energy Performance of Buildings (No. 2) Bill (Bill 150 2021-22) contains the following wording in section 3:

> "*3 Mortgage lenders*
>
> *(1) All mortgage lenders must by 31 December 2030 ensure that the average energy performance level of their domestic portfolios is at least EPC Band C.*
>
> *(2) The Secretary of State may by regulations require mortgage lenders to—*
>
> *(a) provide him or her with information regarding the energy performance of properties in their portfolio; and*
>
> *(b) comply with this section.*"

As discussed in detail in Chapter 2, paragraph 2.3.3 however, this Bill has stalled in parliament and anticipating where it might ultimately end up is no mean feat.

In the meantime however ubiquitous reporting documentation for funders is making steps towards catering directly for sustainability issues. On 10 May 2023, the eight edition of the City of London Law Society (CLLS) long form Certificate of Title was published by the Land Law Committee of the CLLS after a wide-ranging consultation. It was released alongside various updated supplemental documents, such as the wrapper for a report on title, and was broadly very well-received.

What's most interesting here is the seemingly inevitable direction of travel, as signposted by this eighth edition. It does not actually require broad reporting on green leases clauses, but it does pick up on data sharing requirements (which it explains are "perhaps the most important and regularly encountered green lease provision."[22] – see Chapter 4, paragraph 4.3 for notes on drafting this clause). There were also changes to environmental statements, and while consideration by reporting practitioners on climate change risks is generally carved out, this can be of little comfort where those risks are actually disclosed by standard environmental, flood and ground stability searches. In this circumstance, of course, the borrower's solicitors will still have a duty to disclose anything material that is revealed (and may need to provide the funder with reliance on third party reports). See Chapter 6 for discussion on the developing duty in this regard. Ultimately however, there is now clear space for a lender whose key financing metrics include ESG issues, to raise enquiries and insist on reporting more fully.

## 3.3 Understanding the challenges and risks of green leases

It is worth noting, briefly, that there are various reputational, legal and commercial risks attendant in green lease adoption.

22 CLLS Notes, p.7 and p.20

Anticipating problems in these areas will be key to avoiding or overcoming them.

### 3.3.1 Greenwashing

Against the constantly evolving legal and regulatory landscape, and depending on how a company communicates to the market and the public on its use of green leases (and other initiatives), there are risks of being accused of greenwashing. Navigating this concept and the contextual nuances of greenwashing is not easy, but effectively it is broadly agreed to involve a company using (and spending money on) advertising and public messaging to appear more environmentally sustainable than it really is.

An accusation of greenwashing has largely long been a reputational risk, but more recently it is also a legal one. In the UK, misleading environmental claims made directly to consumers are governed by the Consumer Protection from Unfair Trading Regulations 2008 (and soon the enactment of the Digital Markets, Competition and Consumers Bill 2023); business-to-business claims are meanwhile controlled by the Business Protection from Misleading Marketing Regulations 2008. With this focusing the mind, it is important that any company embarking on a sustainability strategy is alive to the issues and committed to follow through on its claims.

Historically, it seems fair to say that early attempts to paint leases green were not much challenged or analysed. Moving forward however, it could be possible that a landlord or tenant looking to benefit from communicating its commitment to green leasing is ready to defend how effective the clauses actually are. Much of the language in the precedent drafting examples that follow in Chapter 4 is indeed non-binding, designed to encourage working together, not mandate it. Perhaps in the future, green lease obligations would generally be better framed using SMART targets (Specific, Measurable, Achievable, Relevant, and Time-

Bound) as this will make it easier to evidence success. Perhaps they should be backed by robust enforcement (see Chapter 4, paragraph 9.1 to 9.4 for more on this idea). At this stage of market transformation, a focus on co-operation is an entirely reasonable approach to encourage take up, but users will need to be careful to frame the narrative properly if they are using green leases to evidence green successes.

For completeness, alongside the legal risk of greenwashing, there is the reputational risk of "green hushing", when companies purposely omit important (negative) environmental information in their reporting or statements.

### 3.3.2 Pressure on relationships in an FRI context

When it comes to drafting leases generally, commercial parties in England and Wales enjoy all the benefits and all the challenges of freedom of contract. Of course, that's not to suggest that practice and custom doesn't dictate certain essentials, and in the commercial real estate world, practitioners are consequently well versed in the principles of a full repairing and insuring (**FRI**) lease. This model, predicated on providing the landlord with a clear quarterly income stream, is possible only because the occupational costs are passed wholesale to the tenant. For decades then, leasing parties have wrangled over the tensions between costs coverage for the landlord and operational freedom for the tenant; the interests of both parties have been fundamentally divergent.

And where they aren't looking to reach the vaulted ceiling of an institutionally acceptable FRI instrument, landlords and tenants are free to commit to covenants on a very low floor indeed.

Unlike in various other jurisdictions[23], the law does not prescribe the structure or contents of a commercial lease. It will not protect the landlord with an implied right of forfeiture, and it has never (yet) allowed a tenant to frustrate a bad deal. There are small legislative tweaks, to notions of landlord consent for example, but the fundamentals are fair game. It's each party for itself. And that includes the planet – contract law certainly doesn't prescribe hurdles and wording to protect the environment.

In many ways then, a green lease is a sea-change not just for the FRI leasing model, but leasing practice overall. Into this potentially antagonistic world, and into those commercial leases that remain predicated on FRI principles, green lease clauses are asking the parties to work together and *share* – ideas, data and ambitions. They ask for operational transparency. For commitment to strategies that transcend the bricks and mortar. The creation of truly sustainable lease product demands a fundamental reframing of leasing practice, somehow *without* undermining its general importance to the commercial real estate investment industry.

Green leases are not the first attempt to shift the dial on the FRI model, but they might benefit from what amounts to a perfect storm of challenges in recent years. In the past, aligned interests were arguably evident in retail turnover rents as, theoretically, healthy sales meant higher rents. The old tensions were still there however, and it was getting harder to draft as technology blurred operational boundaries between real and online worlds. Nonetheless, some landlords are now approaching their tenants as customers. Commentators refer to this as the "operationalization" of real estate, pointing for example to a more

23 In the EU, for example, EC Directive 93/13 obliges member states to introduce protections for contractual partners facing unfair terms and conditions.

hands on approach to landlording in the student housing sector. A recent spate of high-profile insolvencies have meanwhile buffeted a retail sector already reeling from rocketing energy costs and Covid-19 restrictions, leaving landlords able to tell a story about how, when they were prepared to share the pain, they are also able to evidence combined commercial survival.

Ultimately, what greater example of this focus on sustainable survival than in the benefits of environmental co-operation? There is undoubtedly going to be pressure on the parties involved as they morph leasing practice to accommodate these new demands. In this context, where negotiations are not handled well, and where the goals and benefits are not aligned, there is a risk that drafting is only acceded to with suspicion or cynicism, and genuine impact is almost certain to fail.

### 3.3.3 Data

Burgeoning proptech products and the data requirements of ESG management mean that real estate companies used to dealing with bricks and mortar are being expected to pivot into understanding their responsibilities as data controllers. While the legal complexities of collecting and using with data are introduced in Chapter 2, paragraph 2.5.3, the practical challenges are discussed in Chapter 4, paragraph 4.3.

## 3.4 Available tools to help draft Green Leases

In addition to understanding the legal and regulatory backdrop and its trajectory (as discussed in detail in Chapter 2), real estate practitioners have access to a number of excellent tools in order to support, prompt and generate tailored green lease drafting. All of the resources and toolkits discussed below are easily and freely available to assist with creating a bespoke green lease template for your client. Examples of various clauses are picked out for consideration in Chapter 4.

### 3.4.1 The Better Buildings Partnership (BBP) Green Lease Toolkit

https://www.betterbuildingspartnership.co.uk/green-lease-toolkit

The Better Buildings Partnership (BBP) was at the vanguard of the Green Lease drafting opportunity, spotting the need "to improve the sustainability of existing commercial building stock" some fifteen years ago. A not-for-profit collaboration of the UK's leading commercial property owners, BBP first created and published its Green Lease Toolkit in 2008, around the time of that ground-breaking Climate Change Act 2008, with the intention of making model form clauses freely available to dip in and out of. This toolkit was last updated a decade ago in April 2013, and remains one of the most well-known and well-respected green lease tools.

BBP's focus is very much on promulgating non-prescriptive, best practice recommendations for working together, and from its toolkit comes an early definition of what exactly a green lease is: "*A green lease is a standard form lease with additional clauses included which provide for the management and improvement of the Environmental Performance of a building by both owner and occupier(s). Such a document is legally binding and its provisions remain in place for the duration of the term. Green leases tend to be relevant only in the context of leases of commercial buildings.*"

BBP is strictly not aiming to be a certification body. Instead it has, over the years, focused on generating and facilitating collaborative dialogue on green leases in the commercial real estate world. It listens as much as it teaches and, reflecting the increasing ambitions of its users, has been working on an updated toolkit, which is due for publication in 2024. Continuing its strong focus on providing best practice guidance rather than prescription, the new incarnation of the Green Lease Toolkit is being created as a living tool; a dynamic web-based repository of clauses that gives users guidance, including on ten areas that represent a "minimum expectation" for what a green lease ought to contain.

Drafting will now be presented with shades of green ratings (more on the usefulness of grading later in paragraph 3.4.8) and, importantly, the parties using the clauses are asked to engage with "statements of intent", with the intention that they anchor ambitions before becoming bogged down in the minutia of drafting. Furthermore, a roadmap will set out BBP's future ambitions for drafting areas as the concepts of green leasing evolve. Where clauses in the Green Lease Toolkit are discussed in Chapter 4, it is important to be clear that the discussion refers to the extent 2013 publication.

As part of its Green Lease Toolkit, BPP also publish a model Memorandum of Understanding (more on this concept in Chapter 5, paragraph 7.2) and it has also developed the Real Estate Environmental Benchmark (REEB), which it describes as "one of the only benchmarks based on the performance of buildings 'in-use'" (energy, carbon, water and waste performance data)".

### 3.4.2 The Chancery Lane Project (TCLP)

https://chancerylaneproject.org/

The Chancery Lane Project (TCLP) is a collaborative initiative of international legal professionals that creates new contractual clauses to incorporate into precedents and agreements, focused on the delivery of climate solutions. A relative newcomer, being established in 2019, TCLP has made extraordinary inroads to legal and commercial practice in a few short years. At the time of writing, the TCLP website tallies its collaborative input to date: 3,600 professionals, across 350 participating organisations and 113 countries.

In keeping with its commitment to political and professional neutrality, individual clauses are not attributed to any particular firm or lawyer, thus ensuring they remain independent. In fact, the incredible idea behind TCLP is to create a space for innovative cross-fertilisation. In a global geopolitical context largely absent of stringent top-down government regulation on climate change mitigation and adaptation, TCLP empowers lawyers to change the world from the bottom up; on changing how we produce, consume and operate the law.

Each clause is given a child's name, ostensibly to remind users of the next generation who will benefit most from the use of new TCLP clauses in contracts today. Unsurprisingly then, the drafting is focused on maximising impact, although it is published as a free-to-use and adapt resource. This is a realistic approach as the market transforms to address the climate emergency, however as a starter for ten, TCLP drafting is undoubtably "the best attempt to align legal norms with environmental imperatives"[24].

In the context of green leases, TCLP points to several ready-to-use clauses that are available to help with drafting and conversations:

- *Hannah's Clause* – Green Service Charge Provisions
- *Aatmay's Clause* – Repairs and Alterations

[24] This quote was taken from Stephen Brenninkjmeider, Chair of European Climate Foundation ECF, who was speaking at the TCLP Plenary Session (2nd Annual Hackathon) on 5 November 2020.

- *Rosie's Clause* – Alteration/Improvement Provisions
- *Lotta's Clause* – Renewable Electricity
- *Emma's Clause* – Green Residential Lease Clauses can be adapted for commercial leases.
- *Amelie & Lauri's Clause* – this Irish Green Lease can be adapted for E&W.
- You could also consider adapting:
    - *Matthew's Clause* – Late Payment
    - *Alice's Clause* – Single Use Plastic
    - Obligations regarding the tenant having to source products locally
    - *Raphael's Questionnaire* – A Climate Change DDQ, with questions on sustainable travel plans, provision of shower facilities/bike racks, etc
    - Drafting obliging the parties to execute electronically.

### 3.4.3 Model Commercial Lease (MCL)

https://modelcommerciallease.co.uk/leases/

The Model Commercial Lease (MCL) needs little introduction to a readership of commercial property lawyers in England and Wales. Devised as a client led project, originally commissioned by the British Property Federation (BPF), the MCL has been available online for free download and customisation since its launch in 2014 and has enjoyed considerable success in streamlining leasing documents and negotiations. The MCL is periodically updated, lastly in June 2021.

The current incarnation of the MCL includes a sustainability schedule, with drafting generally on co-operation between landlord and tenant in order to improve the environmental performance of property. It provides for the establishment of an environmental forum and the sharing of relevant data. There is relatively standard ancillary drafting on EPCs and environmental performance in the context of alterations. And all of these provisions are considered in Chapter 4.

The green provisions in the MCL are "not intended to impose onerous obligations in relation to sustainability issues but [are] intended to facilitate a discussion between the parties about these issues". This is entirely in keeping with its general ambition to cut out much of the unnecessary negotiation on routine lease grants, and to ensure the parties can get on with addressing the issues that matter most to clients. The ambition is similar to that of BBP, and drafting for the new incarnation of the latter's Green Lease Toolkit has involved working with MCL architects (as well as TCLP).

### 3.4.4 NHS model green lease for commercial premises

https://www.england.nhs.uk/publication/model-form-green-lease-clauses-template/

Reflecting the fact that the "nature of buildings, organisational ambitions and landlord-tenant relationships differ across the NHS", NHS England has produced its own suite of green clauses. It published these in June 2022 as part of its *Estates technical guidance*, making them available and free to use for organisations at any stage of their own green journey.

Designed together with law firm Bevan Brittan, and broadly based on BBP's Green Lease Toolkit documents, the NHS explained that its 2022 suite was tailored to aid with issues that had arisen since BBP's clauses were first drafted fifteen years earlier, e.g. data sharing and net zero carbon targets (such as the NHS has).

The NHS also helpfully categorises its clauses as light green or dark green, to aid with ease of use (more on the usefulness of grading later in paragraph 3.4.8). Its drafted Green Clauses deal with:

- Rent and Rent Reviews
- Repairs
- Alterations
- Alienation
- Energy Obligations
- Environmental Management
- Service Charge

### 3.4.5 Green Lease Leaders (GLL)

https://www.greenleaseleaders.com/green-lease-library

Green Lease Leaders (GLL) is actually US-based but it has ambitions to set global standards. It operates as a three-year recognition program for those who integrate green leasing into their standard practices, and are thus eligible to be awarded Silver, Gold, and/or Platinum badges. It recruits partner advocates to spread awareness and provide case studies that highlight how the GLL clauses are used in practice.

Its freely published resources amount to two comprehensive reference guides: one for tenants and one for landlords, both of which think specifically about sustainability and energy-efficiency. A key aim of GLL is also to try, in the language of its website, to break down the "split incentive barrier". This effectively means understanding the importance of aligning the financial and environmental benefits of green clauses so that they speak to both landlord and tenant parties. "Performance-based lease language," it says, "fosters collaboration between landlords and tenants." In the absence of sticks, this means highlighting the carrots.

### 3.4.6 Institute for Market Transformation (IMT)

https://www.imt.org/resources/green-lease-language-examples/?

The Institute for Market Transformation (IMT) is another US non-profit initiative, that aims to "bridge[s] the intersection of business, government, and community priorities to spotlight business practices and advance public policy to improve U.S. buildings." The stakes are high, as IMT explains, the real estate sector "can play a critical role in accelerating the transformation of the U.S. economy [... to] prioritize local wealth and community." And its ambitions are accordingly lofty ("to ensure that everyone in the U.S. benefits from high-performing buildings in all facets of their lives") but its approach is nonetheless consciously non-partisan, and involves working on co-creating projects with capacity for scale within the fields of public policy and business practices.

Importantly for this book, IMT published its own example green clauses online in January 2023, and these are ready to be incorporated and amended at will. IMT clauses are unsurprisingly US-focused when it comes to referencing common standards or laws, but the ideas are wide-ranging and worth being aware of. IMT also signposts visitors to the Green Lease Leaders tools. Its website is clear that "energy-aligned leases" can break down barriers between landlords and tenants in efficiently designed and operated spaces.

### 3.4.7 Considering the requirements of benchmarking tools – e.g. the Global Real Estate Sustainability Benchmark (GRESB)

https://www.gresb.com/nl-en/

*"By industry, for industry"*

The Global Real Estate Sustainability Benchmark (GRESB) is an industry-led provider of transparent, validated and standardised ESG data to financial markets. Established in 2009, it's a member-based organisation which aims to support investors integrating ESG data into their investment decisions. As discussed in Chapter 2, paragraph 2.7, the real estate market has long been setting its own targets for ESG benchmarking, and GRESB calculates that this means it is now directly catering for 98% of investors. Accordingly, its website claims it "is trusted by 170 institutional investors and more than 2,200 fund managers, companies and asset operators".

Of course, GRESB is not strictly a drafting tool, but it is included in this section because, depending on the landlord's drivers behind its need for green leasing, this tool effectively lays out clearly what might be expected by corporate investors who are looking to make an ESG-sound investment. In order to benchmark organisations, GRESB delivers a granular questionnaire that explores various areas of that company's operations, effectively enabling it to earn rating points for dealing overtly with (or requesting that a counter party engages with) various green issues.

In asking whether an entity includes ESG-specific requirements in its standard lease contracts therefore, GRESB assessors are looking for evidence of things like: environmental initiatives; the enabling of upgrade works; ESG management collaboration; energy, waste and water management; Indoor environmental quality management; sustainable procurement and transport options etc. Where a standard approach to its leasing does not cater for any of these identified issues then, a landlord might spot an opportunity to draft with this in mind in the future.

In fact, interestingly for "green" leasing, when considering its list of Real Estate ESG questions, it's easy to see how GRESB's ESG focus often goes well beyond green in the traditional sense. That S limb of ESG, and the potential for social initiatives to fit within a commercial leasing arrangement, is considered in Chapter 4, paragraphs 4.16 to 4.22. Of course, some of these ESG preoccupations belong more to another document such as an operational building manual (this is discussed further in Chapter 5, paragraph 5.3).

### 3.4.8 Nifty shades of green

It is clear from the analysis of the different drafting tools available that there is already, and there will certainly be in the future, considerable co-operation and cohesion when it comes to the entities and initiatives setting a new green lease standard. This fact is an essential part of driving transformation in the commercial real estate sector. Coalescence on the ideas and obligations empowers negotiators and speeds transactions, ultimately reducing costs for clients and ensuring broader take up.

Another key tool for take-up is clarity over where a drafted clauses sits on the scale between easy drafting win and ambitious practical impact. When it comes to assessing the way the general real estate market is likely to perceive the impact of the drafting options or ambitions, most will therefore tend to refer to a clause or suite being on a spectrum between light green and dark green.

Light green provisions are considerably less onerous on the contracting parties. These clauses perhaps allow for minor changes to be made to how tenants use and occupy buildings, but they usually don't allocate responsibility for costs or even require financial outlay. These are entry-level clauses, allowing commercial entities to dip their toe in carbon reduction schemes, but there is a focus on the partnership and aspiration. As between the parties, there be no hard consequences for breach.

At the other end of the spectrum, dark green clauses are ambitious in scope and usually work to help landlord or tenant companies achieve compliance with articulated ESG priorities or carbon reduction targets. By laying absolute requirements on the parties, the clauses tend to require some degree of financial outlay. The NHS explains that its dark green interventions are created to "allow organisations to focus on more substantial interventions". Dark green drafting is less likely to be the subject of any greenwashing accusation (see paragraph 3.3.1), although thought should always be given to enabling the parties agree on the implementation and monitoring of absolute covenants, with a view to understanding consequences for breach.

In reality, at this stage in the journey to green leases becoming industry standard, most clauses that make their way into completed documents will be at the lighter end of drafting. It is not uncommon however for companies which have set specific corporate targets or goals, to insist on particular dark green mechanisms (such as a pre-approved consent for installing photovoltaic panels). Most green leases will select both light and dark green provisions from between the available templates, to reflect the ambitions and targets of the parties involved.

# CHAPTER FOUR

# DRAFTING THE GREEN LEASE

As already discussed, at this point in time, there is no institutionally accepted market standard for what constitutes a green lease. That's not to say however that the contents of this new generation of green lease provisions haven't coalesced around particular themes. A green lease will typically contain some or all the following clauses, which will be incorporated to varying degrees of detail and ambition. Let's take a closer look at seven main themes which can be used to craft relevant green leases clauses.

By grouping drafting initiatives together with notes and commentary, this chapter puts green drafting in the context of standard leasing practice as well as its new environmental rationale. Little surprise then that the sector, looking to create green leases as a new generation of tools in the battle for decarbonisation, is necessarily defining its own goals and standards.

It's worth saying of course that in relation to all the clauses set out and discussed below, where drafting is suggested or replicated from the tools and playbooks described in Chapter 3, always refer back to the original source where it is referenced. These are living tools and will be updated over time. In particular, references to the BBP Green Lease Toolkit are to the 2013 incarnation of this product, which is extent at time of writing, but which is to be updated shortly. See Chapter 3, paragraph 3.4.1 for more information.

Also remember that while the drafting is intended to slot into and work with your existing lease document, standard leasing elements such as the interpretation and definitions have been largely omitted, to avoid the content becoming unwieldy. The appropriate definitions will likely need amendment therefore, and defined terms generally are placed inside square brackets.

Relying heavily on the freely available drafting toolkits detailed in Chapter 3, this chapter considers clauses as they currently and as they could exist, and has organised these broadly into seven themes:

- THEME 1 – Working together to improve a building's environmental performance
- THEME 2 – Meeting statutory and regulatory requirements
- THEME 3 – Costs sharing and recovery for energy initiatives and improvements
- THEME 4 – Amendments to standard tenant covenants
- THEME 5 – Amendments to Landlord rights and reservations
- THEME 6 – Additional new tenant covenants
- THEME 7 – Remedies and enforcement on breach

## Theme 1 – Working together to improve a building's environmental performance

### 4.1 General duties of co-operation

First and foremost, the green lease is often marked out by the fact that together, both landlord and tenant are seeking to create an expectation that they will at least consider, and at best promote and improve, the environmental performance of the building and/or their corporate impact on climate change.

An overarching commitment to co-operation can be detailed and documented in a variety of different ways.

This example confirmatory clause for general co-operation on asset impact between the landlord and the tenant is set out in the BBP Green Lease Toolkit:

> *The [Landlord] and the [Tenant]*
>
> *a) Confirm that [wherever reasonably practicable] they wish to promote and improve the [Environmental Performance] of the [Premises] and the [Building]*
>
> *b) Agree [in good faith but without legal obligation] to cooperate with each other to identify appropriate strategies for the improvement of the [Environmental Performance] of the [Premises] and the [Building]*

Similarly, additional recitals can be used to confirm common intention and even refer to specific targets set as part of a party's corporate objectives. The following is taken from Aatmay's Clause (TCLP):

> *A. The Landlord and Tenant [have signed up to the [Race to Zero] and] acknowledge their common intention to:*
>
> (i) *achieve their respective organisational net zero targets; and*
>
> (ii) *align with the objectives of the [Paris Agreement] (in particular pursuing efforts to limit global temperature increase to 1.5 degrees Celsius above pre-industrial levels*

*and achieving net zero or net negative emissions by 2050 or sooner)*

B. *The Landlord and Tenant agree to pursue (A) in a manner that promotes a just transition to a low carbon economy and results in at least a [7%] reduction of greenhouse gas emissions year on year.*

Notes on using these clauses:

4.1.1 *Non-binding obligations*

***Is there any point to an obligation to consider an agreement to agree?***

Legally, of course, an agreement to agree is never enforceable. At worst then, a statement of intended co-operation that requires a later agreement without a mechanism for resolution risks being entirely without purpose. Similarly, agreeing to consider is not actual agreement on anything.

Incorporating this wording is no pyrrhic victory however. It's a Trojan horse when it comes to setting a tone for conversation; and foreshadows the very start of a potential pivot for traditional FRI leasing. In setting up a future intention to co-operate and identify strategies, the statement of intent is not legally binding ("wishing to promote" is a relatively simple commitment to incorporate without additional liability) but it is likely to be accepted. BBP's drafting does not fundamentally jeopardise FRI principles then (as an obligation it clearly sits at the light green end of our impact scale), but simply articulating a shared aim can be a powerful tool.

An overarching statement of shared values offers context for a purposive interpretation of other green clauses in the remainder of the lease. It could therefore prove to be of real benefit to a party wanting to enforce a "green" initiative during the life of the lease, or to bring its counterparty to the table to negotiate, or even to seek formal landlord consent in a green context.

Of course, obligations like this one can rely on the covenantor making various shades of endeavour (for example reasonable endeavours or best endeavours). But even then they might be heavily caveated with comfort such as "provided there is no increase in costs" or "so far as practicable". The clear consequences of this are that enforcement is complicated (see paragraphs 4.23 to 4.26).

***Are there any other advantages to the co-operation clause?***

As a side note, if your client is looking to achieve a GRESB rating, for example, points could well be awarded for entering environmental initiatives and ESG management collaboration. A common intention in the lease for collaboration could help evidence this.

RICS' Service Charges In Commercial Property (1st Edition) (first published as guidance in April 2019 and then again in August 2023 as a professional standard) also gave weight to the co-operative approach: "*This professional standard supports and promotes a cooperative and collaborative approach in recognising and managing the environmental impact of the occupation and management of commercial premises.*"

4.1.2 *Essential definitions*

***How do you refer to overarching environmental targets that can underpin co-operation?***

Unless it's couched in broad aspiration terms of later co-operation, it can be difficult to narrow down workable definitions for overarching environmental targets.

The Aatmay's clause recitals offer an opportunity for both parties to incorporate their internally generated / published organisational targets, or other third party or scientific standards. Much will depend on client instruction, but TCLP generally provides useful, ready-made definitions for various objective targets, such as:

> ***Net Zero Target*** *is to reduce and remove [GHG] emissions, including by offsetting [Residual Emissions] (i.e. those emitted after all reasonable efforts have been made to reduce them), to achieve a balance between the sources and sinks of [GHGs].*
>
> ***Science Based Targets*** *are plans reduce [GHG] emissions which are validated and published by the [Science Based Targets initiative (SBTi)]*
>
> ***Carbon Budget*** *is the aggregate of [value] tonnes of [Carbon Dioxide Equivalent] of [GHG] emissions permitted within the period of [x].*
>
> ***Carbon Dioxide Equivalent*** *(CO2e or CO2eq) means the standard metric measure to compare the global warming potential of various [GHGs] over a specified timescale.*

You could alternatively use the concept of an "Efficiency Objective" to be clear that the overarching aim of both parties is to reduce operational GHG emissions from the specific property, or achieve a broader net zero operational target for the property/estate. There is a definition of this in Aatmay's Clause from TCLP:

> ***Efficiency Objective*** *means that, in relation to the occupation, operation and use of the [Property][Premises], the parties will work together to:*
>
> *(a) maximise energy efficiency in the [Property][Premises];*

> *(b) achieve the sustainability performance targets of the [Landlord's][Tenant's] sustainability linked loan;]*
>
> *(c) reduce the GHG Emissions associated with the [Property][Premises] to help the parties achieve their Net Zero Targets;*
>
> *(d) [Offset any Residual Emissions related to the [Property][Premises];]*
>
> *(e) use sustainable materials and avoid the use of materials that increase the Embedded Carbon;*
>
> *(f) reuse and recycle materials to ensure that they are salvaged or otherwise saved from landfill;*
>
> *(g) adopt environmentally friendly working methods, including minimising energy use through plant and site services;*
>
> *(h) protect and enhance existing ecological features on site;*
>
> *(i) minimise air (dust and fumes) and noise pollution;*
>
> *(j) minimise water use;*
>
> *(k) use local suppliers; [and]*
>
> *(l) promote green travel to and from the site (including walking, cycling or using public transport).*

***How do you define Environmental Performance in relation to an individual property?***

Clearly the exact definition of Environmental Performance is necessarily asset specific, and will often refer to the operational nuances on the ground.

As a starter for ten, for example, the **MCL** uses a very broad catch all for every measurable "in" and "out":

> *"**Environmental Performance**" means all or any of the following:*
>
> *(a) the consumption of energy and associated generation of greenhouse gas emissions;*
>
> *(b) the consumption of water;*
>
> *(c) waste generation and management; and*
>
> *(d) any other environmental impact arising from the use or operation of the Premises;*

Aatmay's Clause from TCLP meanwhile includes a more detailed definition, from which relevant measures can be selected in the context of any specific property:

> ***Environmental Performance** means the extent to which the [negative] environmental impacts and GHG Emissions of the Property and/or the Building (including its component parts) during manufacture, occupation, operation, use and disposal have been mitigated [and the positive environmental impacts of the Property and/or the Building promoted]. Such impacts include (but are not limited to) those arising from:*
>
> - *the sources of materials and how such materials are sourced (including materials containing Embedded Carbon and materials sourced using Sustainable Procurement);*
> - *the use, recycling and re-use of materials [used in repairs, renewals, fitting out and replacements];*
> - *the type and efficiency of energy sources (including the percentage of Renewable Energy Sources as a proportion of all energy sources supplying the Property and/or the Building);*
> - *the rate and efficiency of energy consumption;*

- *water sources (including availability of alternative sources of water (including treated water, rainwater and Greywater);*
- *the [quantity/ rate] and efficiency of water consumption [and discharge];*
- *resilience to the impacts of climate change;*
- *[pollution and] waste processing, including the rate or efficiency of waste recycling or re-use of resources;*
- *methods of transport of supplies and people to and from the Property;*
- *Biodiversity and Natural Capital;*
- *deconstruction and disposal; and*
- *any other matter which relates to occupation, operation and use of the Property and/or the Building and the Environment,*

*in each case taking into account any Adverse Climate Effects resulting from changes in the use or intensity of use of the Property and/or the Building.*

***Is your environmental performance target measurable?***

If your target is one of Environmental Performance and linked to the operation of a specific property asset, it should be possible to chart how it is directly affected by the behaviour of the leasing parties. And in that case, measuring and reporting against that target should ultimately be achievable for the landlord or tenant. If the energy draw goes up, for example, the Environmental Performance target could be missed and there is therefore incentive not to leave the lights on.

Referring, like in Aatmay's clause, to an overarching corporate target is going to make measurement considerably harder. Do these targets need a deadline, and how can progress even be measured within a lease term? What is a realistic deadline anyway to achieve targets such as net zero? In the context of the lease, the value of this clause is undoubtedly then in the scene setting discussed in paragraph 4.1.1.

### 4.1.3 *Impact on the traditional FRI leasing model*

***How does a duty of co-operation sit within conventional commercial leasing practice?***

A large part of the green lease drafting challenge is giving the goals of efficiency and sustainability the best chance of success within the UK's long-established FRI commercial leasing practice. A standard lease will typically contain well-trodden clauses, and yet many new green lease or ESG provisions can effectively upend this status quo. They are detail heavy, operationally-focused and not, frankly, in their natural home. Even where ambition for a genuinely sustainable asset is shared between the parties, targets must be achievable, covenants clear and obligations impactful.

The creation of truly sustainable lease product, with its emphasis on co-operation and proactive joint management, demands a fundamental reframing of traditional FRI practice. To put this co-operation clause in context then, it is worth considering how far it is even possible to align the interests of landlords and tenants within the standard leasing practice of FRI. More discussion on this point is set out in Chapter 3, paragraph 3.3.2.

### 4.1.4 *Competition law*

***Are there valid concerns for corporate co-operation under competition law?***

This is discussed in more detail in Chapter 2, paragraph 2.5.1.

## 4.2 Creation of a shared forum

Once the parties agree to the principle of co-operation on environmental initiatives and/or shared corporate targets, it is sensible to provide opportunities for further discussion and review during the course of the lease term. Establishing a forum is particularly useful in the context of an estate asset or multi-tenanted building, where the landlord wants to engage and agree strategies with multiple tenants – broad buy-in after all will be essential to their success.

To do this, the MCL sets out in its sustainability schedule an example clause for the establishment of a shared environmental forum between landlord and tenant (very similar drafting for establishing a Building Management Group is available in the BBP Green Lease Toolkit):

> 1 *The [Landlord] [may][must] provide an environmental forum (the "**Forum**") that will meet on a regular basis to:*
>
> 1.1 *consider the adequacy and improvement of data sharing on energy and water use, waste production and recycling;*
>
> 1.2 *review the Environmental Performance of the Premises;*
>
> 1.3 *agree targets and strategies for a travel plan for travelling to and from the Premises; and*
>
> 1.4 *agree targets and strategies to improve the [Environmental Performance] of the Premises.*
>
> 2 *The Forum may take any form that affords an appropriate means of communication and exchange of views, whether by meeting in person or not.*
>
> 3 *The [Landlord] and the [Tenant] will each nominate a suitable person to participate in the Forum. They will try to ensure that their nominees attend and participate in any*

*Forum meetings or discussions of which appropriate advance notice has been given.*

4 *[The [Landlord] and the [Tenant] may agree to allow third parties to participate in the Forum for a specified period or for a specified purpose.]*

5 *[The [Landlord] will try to ensure that a representative of any managing agents appointed by the [Landlord] attends and participates in any Forum meetings or discussions of which appropriate advance notice has been given.]*

6 *Where any of the issues considered, reviewed or agreed in the Forum relate exclusively to the [Premises], either the [Landlord] or the [Tenant] may request that these are discussed between them and their authorised agents only (and not with any other permitted participants in the Forum).*

Notes on using this clause:

4.2.1 *Non-binding obligations*

***What is the forum expected to achieve?***

Beyond setting up a forum, always consider what exactly the parties are hoping to achieve through it. This light green drafting does not at the outset require much more than the creation of a safe space for sharing ideas on environmental targets and strategies taking place at the property. Is the idea just to allow for an informal exchange of views? Discussing strategies after all is not agreeing them, and the drafting of the clause permits a rather informal exchange of opinions without even requiring resolutions to be recorded in minutes.

Like the light green notions of co-operation, there is some strength in this drafting however. At the outset, the creation of a shared forum on these terms is unlikely to be controversial or onerous, and it clearly supports the shared cooperation goal discussed in paragraph 4.1. The hope appears to be that the existence of such a forum will focus minds periodically and organically drive more co-operation, which is clearly a good thing.

Where possible however, depending of course on client instruction (perhaps the landlord already runs a successful forum on an estate or multi-let building and wants to guarantee future involvement by all relevant parties), there is space here to tighten the requirements. Perhaps you could strengthen its remit, by referencing particular already established strategies or shared goals, or set minimum expectations on the regime of meetings, e.g. quarterly, or annually? Should they be in-person or online?

It's clearly important that the parties "try and ensure" their representatives are available to attend the forum, but what happens if they don't attend? Consideration of the consequences of green clause breach is at paragraphs 4.23 to 4.26.

### 4.2.2 *Confidentiality*

***Are the parties concerned about keeping discussions in the forum private?***

Much of the content of a forum is likely to be related to the operational behaviour of the parties, and it is easy to see how attendees might be worried about inadvertently committing to new environmental strategies, or admitting fault for a failure to meet targets, especially in front of the landlords or, for example on a retail park, competitors. This clause attempts to alleviate some of these concerns by allowing the parties to request that some conversations are effectively taken offline.

Effective discussions are fairly likely at times to require the involvement of third parties however, such as the managing agent. The drafting of this clause does therefore anticipate that these parties are permitted for a specified period/purpose.

In the content of an FRI leasing model however, which predicated on allocating operational costs to a tenant (more on this in Chapter 3, paragraph 3.3.2), a forum will need to work hard to ensure landlords and tenants share information freely and openly. This only highlights the importance of what GLL calls the "split incentive barrier": both landlords and tenants will need to understand and witness the value of these meetings.

## 4.3 Duties to share data and information

*What isn't measured, isn't managed.* With this mantra it is easy to see the importance of collecting and understanding data relevant to any environmental targets. Data is essential at the outset of any sustainability journey, to set a building's internal benchmark and to design appropriate targets, and later, to assess the effectiveness and success of those goals and strategies.

Many green leases therefore incorporate provisions aimed at ensuring data, on things like utilities consumption, is shared between landlords and tenants.

This drafting came from the BBP Green Lease Toolkit, but there is very similar drafting in the NHS Green Clauses and the MCL):

> 1. *The [Landlord] and the [Tenant] will share the [Environmental Performance Data] they hold relating to the [Premises] and/or the [Building]. This [Environmental Performance Data] will be shared on a regular basis [but not less frequently than monthly/quarterly/annually] with each other, with [the Managing Agent] and with any third party*

*who the [Landlord] and the [Tenant] agree needs to receive such data.*

2. *Save where they are under a statutory obligation of disclosure, the [Landlord] and the [Tenant] will keep confidential the [Environmental Performance Data] shared under this clause, and will only use such data for the purposes of:*
    a. *monitoring and improving the [Environmental Performance] of the [Premises] and/or the [Building]; and/or*
    b. *measuring the [Environmental Performance] of the [Premises] and/or the [Building] against any agreed targets.*

*The [Landlord] will ensure that the [Managing Agent] is placed under a similar obligation to that set out in clause [] to keep any shared data confidential and to use it only for the purposes listed in that clause.*

*Where the [Landlord] or [Tenant] discloses any shared data to a third party, they will procure that that third party is placed under a similar obligation to that set out in clause [ ] to keep any shared data confidential and to use it only for the purposes listed in that clause.*

Notes on using this clause:

4.3.1 Mutuality of obligations

***What is the purpose of the data to be shared?***

There is already a mutuality to this loose covenant to share data and information, in that the data may be generated by either landlord or tenant. Always ensure however that the data to be shared and received will be useful. Some parties could arguably make more use of the relevant data set. Could it be used to create and measure the impact of an environmental strategies, or could it be used to achieve benchmarking points as part of a separate corporate initiative? A tenant measuring the performance of its business is more likely to rely on its own data and not the landlord's, for example.

For this clause to work most effectively, much comes down to the definition of what constitutes the relevant data. The MCL has the simplest approach here – it is the data that relates to Environmental Performance (see paragraph 4.1.2).

*What about confidentiality? How does data get re-bundled and reshared?*

When it comes to sharing any collected data further than the landlord and tenant parties, this clause permits third party disclosure to the managing agents and any other third party the landlord and tenant can agree on.

There may be good reasons however for sharing performance data beyond those directly involved in the management of the relevant property. Recognised industry bodies engaged in benchmarking/ sustainability standards might need access to the data (see Chapter 3, paragraph 3.4.7 on GRESB). It's even conceivable that a landlord or tenant could want to use the data to encourage and promote sustainability within the real estate sector as a whole.

There are additional considerations however for a multi-tenanted building or on an estate. A tenant here is almost certain to expect similar obligations on data sharing to be present in other leases, so that a full picture is given. But once that data reaches the landlord, it could conceivably form part of the *Environmental Performance Data* it holds and is then expected to be shared on a regular basis with other tenants.

Will each tenant be happy for such data to be shared between its peers, via the landlord? Some will be concerned that such data could effectively be used against them. A tenant causing a large energy draw in communal areas could for example need to defend a lop-sided service charge split, or another tenant could face penalty if its behaviour is highlighted as undermining shared environmental targets.

### *Is any energy data personal?*

In collating and sharing data, both parties must also be very clear about their own obligations under data protection law. For more information on this point, see Chapter 2, paragraph 2.5.3. Your lease document may already contain provisions setting out obligations to comply with data protection legislation, but do note that the data is likely to need generally to be properly anonymised, so that no personal data can be ascertained amongst shared data sets.

Any equipment installed for the collection or measurement of real time energy data must therefore be set up in such a way that personal data is protected. In an office environment, for example, it's possible that heating or aircon in a small room can be calibrated for routine occupation by one person, with the result that their personal behaviour can be tracked via energy data from smart metres and breaker boxes.

By way of a cautionary tale in this broad area, a high-profile case in Germany in October 2019 saw real estate company Deutsche Wohnen SE fined 14.5m for breaching data protection law. The company had been storing tenants' personal data without a legal basis (Article 6, GDPR) and had failed to implement the GDPR principle of privacy by design (Articles 5 and 25(1), GDPR). Berlin's supervisory authority found obsolete data was not being deleted and there was no internal process for assessment whether storage of personal data was legal or even necessary. At the time, the fine was the highest fine imposed in Germany for these breaches, and while this was clearly based on the EU's GDPR, the Data Protection Act 2018 in England and Wales contains very similar obligations so there are clearly lessons to learn.

### 4.3.2 Clarity of obligations

***When should data be shared?***

In providing for data sharing between the parties, by very clear about when this is expected, and how often, in order to be objectively useful to target setting and measuring. Should data spreadsheets be generated periodically, or on reasonable request? Some data will only actually be available at certain times, or it may mean physically checking a metre. The collection, anonymisation and presentation of data could become onerous.

***How should shared data be standardised?***

Similarly, the data sharing clause above sets no expectations for the standardisation of data delivery; its form is not dictated. But metrics in practice can vary widely, and raw spreadsheets without standardised measurements are likely to be labour intensive to interpret and draw meaningful conclusions from. From a landlord point of view, standardisation is particularly important where the property is multi-let or on an estate. From a tenant point of view, having the form dictated merely pushes down a responsibility to process the raw information.

In the market, attention is being given generally to how real estate sector data can help companies avoid risks and serve society, and a key part of this will be standardisation of data sets. Organisations such as the not-for-profit alliance the RED Foundation are looking specifically at these issues. Undoubtedly, the coming years will see the standardisation of robust, sharable metrics.

### 4.3.3 Corollary rights for installing data collection equipment

***How will the parties collect the necessary data at the property and generate reports to be shared?***

The installation of meters and proptech and sensors that measure environmental factors such as temperature, air quality or energy usage, play a central role in data collection. Of course, it depends entirely on the property and commercial agreement as to which party will be responsible for the installation of such equipment, and for covering the costs of the same.

Corollary rights to install and use might be needed in the lease however and, depending on the set up of the property, attention might be given to the recovery of costs via a service charge. For more information on this, see paragraph 4.6. When it comes to the inconvenience and cost of equipment installation, there are clearly narratives for the relevant parties to tell in respect of how data will deliver tangible benefits.

## Theme 2 – Meeting statutory and regulatory requirements

All parties committed to green principles must also be able to react and adopt to legislative and regulatory change. New targets and strategies might of course be imposed top down on the commercial real estate sector, but for now, as discussed in Chapter 2, that basically means catering for MEES and Energy Performance Certificates (EPCs).

## 4.4 Drafting for MEES

References to EPCs have been a longstanding feature of general commercial leasing, however green leases often consciously extend the practicalities of EPC control. Drafting might therefore seek to limit the creation of EPCs, obligate the maintenance of a particular (standard) rating to protect the landlord's position under MEES or deal with the cost consequences of any energy improvement works recommended throughout the term.

This general EPC clause comes from the MCL. There is very similar drafting in the NHS Green Clauses and the BBP Green Leases Toolkit.

> 1. *The Tenant must not commission an EPC in respect of the Premises unless required to do so by the Energy Performance of Buildings (England and Wales) Regulations 2012. If the Tenant is required to commission an EPC, the Tenant must (at the Landlord's option) commission an EPC from an assessor approved by the Landlord or pay the Landlord's costs of commissioning an EPC for the Premises.*
> 2. *The Tenant must co-operate with the Landlord, so far as is reasonably necessary, to allow the Landlord to commission any EPC for the Premises and:*
>    (a) *provide the Landlord (at the Landlord's cost) with copies of any plans or other information held by the Tenant that would assist in commissioning that EPC; and*
>    (b) *allow such access to the Premises to any energy assessor appointed by the Landlord as is reasonably necessary to inspect the Premises for the purposes of preparing any EPC.*
> 3. *The Tenant must give the Landlord written details on request of the unique reference number of any EPC the Tenant commissions in respect of the Premises.*
> 4. *The Landlord must give the Tenant written details on request of the unique reference number of any EPC the Landlord commissions in respect of the Premises.*

For completeness, the current requirements under MEES, and the likely trajectory for compliance, are set out in Chapter 2, paragraph 2.3.

Notes on using this clause:

4.4.1 *EPC control*

***What extent of control is a landlord able to claim over EPC production and process?***

This clause is essentially all about EPC control, but there are limits to how far that control can extend. Clearly a landlord can't prevent the tenant obtaining an EPC where it is legally obliged to do so (no well-advised tenant would ever agree to this since it would jeopardise its alienation potential), but it can limit commission to those circumstances set out in the clause above.

A landlord might also want to ensure that when an EPC is commissioned, its own nominated assessor is used. This is important, as it the choice of assessor can make a considerable difference to the execution of the examination and the ultimate rating. Non-Domestic Energy Assessors (NDEA) can produce vastly different ratings on the same building, by carrying out different levels of investigation. At the very least, a landlord might want to maintain rights of approval (acting reasonably) over the tenant's selection of assessor.

Note that the exact extent of co-operation requirements here are fairly mutual, such as handing over details of EPC reference numbers in the event the *landlord* wants to commission an EPC over the property.

### 4.4.2 *The process and effects of EPC registration*

***What control might a landlord want in relation to the registration process?***

In the commercial world, it is possible to commission an EPC as a fishing exercise to assess a property's rating while a strategy is set for letting or MEES compliance/exemption. This 'draft' EPC becomes live, and supersedes any previous rating, when it is registered on the PRS Exemptions Register. In this context, drafting for EPC control is all the more important.

This registration nuance is particularly important where a property has an existing rating, in an existing registered EPC, which is actually standard. Where the lease is not in breach of MEES, a tenant's interests will often align with the landlord's (for instance, it will need a standard rating if it plans to sublet). But EPCs last ten years and a new certificate with a lower, substandard rating could conceivably be sought and registered by mistake.

Either way, the landlord will want to avoid finding itself in breach of MEES when a substandard EPC is commissioned without its knowledge. EPC ratings granted a decade or so ago when they were introduced are dropping by an average of two ratings on re-assessment, largely because of improvements in the assessment software. This exercise could easily then jeopardise an existing MEES compliant letting and leave the landlord unwittingly in breach.

In this case, the landlord might want to be able to insist that registration of a new EPC is deferred for a period to allow it to consider improvement recommendations and available exemptions in the breathing space before the draft EPC becomes live.

Note that draft EPCs cannot be obtained in the residential world, however this is a powerful tool for the commercial landlord formulating a letting strategy.

4.4.3 *Dovetailing this clause with other EPC references in the lease*

***Where else in the lease are EPCs referenced?***

A landlord will clearly want to be sure that other clauses in the lease cannot inadvertently (adversely) affect or undermine an existing standard EPC rating. Key clauses for attention with therefore include:

- Alterations (see paragraph 4.11)

- Yield up/determination (see paragraph 4.8)

4.4.4 *Catering for the expected MEES rating trajectory*

***How best to cater for the likely hike in minimum standard EPC ratings?***

When drafting for MEES, remember that a general upwards trajectory in standard ratings must still be expected, albeit that the situation is still incredibly unclear (see Chapter 2, paragraph 2.3.3). This means that a tenant covenant to maintain an EPC rating should avoid referring directly to an E rating, or a B rating, or even whichever standard rating exists at the time of the lease grant. It could better refer to the maintenance of an EPC rating to "*at least such rating as constitutes a minimum standard under The Energy Efficiency (Private Rented Property) (England and Wales) Regulations 2015, as at the date of the EPC is registered.*" Drafting that refers broadly only to not *adversely* affecting the existing rating might not be enough to ensure future compliance.

This is particularly important to avoid being caught out in the context of a lease renewal under the Landlord and Tenant Act 1954. See Chapter 5, paragraph 5.4 for more detail on this.

## Theme 3 – Costs sharing and recovery for energy initiatives and improvements

One way or another, fulfilling the performance targets inherent in a green lease, or meeting EPC rating standards under MEES by carrying out recommended improvement works. is going to cost. There is an argument for the allocation of this cost based on which party is most likely to benefit from the improvement: a tenant may pay lower utility bills for example, or a landlord may benefit from an asset with a higher capital value. In practice though this can involve granular and complex assessment. It's safe to assume then that there will be a debate on costs burden on every new letting, particularly where the benefit will outlive the lease term, or the term covers the key dates at which standard ratings under MEES could be raised.

Depending upon the negotiating power of the parties, any new equipment installation or carrying out of improvement works might be specifically covered in the lease. For example, the parties might draft for specify recovery via the service charge; via a rent hike on review; via the back door, using other cost-sharing or statutory compliance covenants; or even via the yield up provisions. Either way, the cost burden needs to be properly allocated and covered to give environmental targets the best chance of success.

The good news is that the market appears to be moving in the direction that these costs need not be allocated wholesale to one party, but that they may be shared between both. This is another example of how the traditional FRI model is shifting slightly within the context of green leasing.

## 4.5 Recovery of costs via the service charge

There Is almost always a tension on cost allocation when cash is spent on common parts of a multi-let property or estate. The service charge provisions are nonetheless where the majority of landlord expenditure on repairs, maintenance and services is detailed, authorised and recouped. Typically however, unless a commercial lease provides for a sinking or reserve fund, these provisions will not envisage the *replacement* of items unless and until they are beyond economic repair. In this context, money spent on upgrades for efficiency can actually be tricky to recover.

Nonetheless, a landlord keen to comply with regulation or respond to tenant demands for a more efficient, healthier building, might well argue that it is should be able to pass on the costs of achieving the same via the service charge. It might ultimately benefit from a higher property value, but in the meantime, the tenant should be able to enjoy measurable cost savings and be further incentivised to use the property efficiently. Demonstrating that cost saving could of course be relatively straightforward in the current energy crisis.

This drafting comes from Hannah's Clause (TCLP). It takes into account the Royal Institution of Chartered Surveyors' (RICS) Service Charge Statement and Code for Leasing Business Premises (now a professional standard), which encourage cooperation throughout the lease term to ensure the property is used as sustainably as possible:

> *1. Provision of Services*
>
> *1.1 [In relation to a provision that the [Landlord] may add any other measure, facility or service in the interests of good estate management] provided that the [Landlord] shall have due regard to the effect of any such proposed additional measure, facility or service on [Environmental Performance] and shall*

*seek to minimise any adverse effect on [Environmental Performance] where reasonably practicable and where to do so does not impose an undue economic burden on the [Landlord].*

1.2 *[The [Landlord] shall not be required to provide any [Services] which would [in its reasonable opinion] [materially] adversely affect the [Environmental Performance] of the [Property] and/or the [Building].]*

1.3 *In providing the [Services], the [Landlord] shall have due regard to promoting [Environmental Performance]. The [Tenant] acknowledges that, as a consequence, the [Service Costs] may be higher than if the [Landlord] procured the [Services] without due regard to promoting [Environmental Performance]. The [Landlord] shall ensure that any difference in costs is economically proportionate.*

***2. Sustainability***

2.1 *Each of the [Landlord] and [Tenant] shall cooperate to identify and implement appropriate strategies for improving [Environmental Performance]. Nothing in this Part is intended to impose an undue economic burden on the parties or require the parties to agree to terms which are commercially unreasonable.*

2.2 *The [Landlord] shall have due regard to any sufficiently detailed written proposal by the [Tenant] [of/ for inclusion within the [Service Charge]] any measures which are likely to improve [Environmental Performance][(where the costs exceed those of normal maintenance, repair or replacement) or additional service or installation that falls within the definition of an [Excluded Service Costs]], and the [Landlord] shall respond to the [Tenant] within a reasonable period of receiving such proposal with reasons for accepting, rejecting or modifying it (bearing in mind the objective of improving [Environmental Performance]).*

Notes on this clause:

4.5.1 General impact of term lease on recovery of service charge items

***What difference does it make if my tenant is signing up to a short lease?***

Tenants with shorter leases will be less inclined to enable improvement upgrades by virtue of a service charge mechanism they have, in practice, little control over. They will be concerned that they will be paying for or contributing towards upgrades they won't ever actually benefit from. They may also reject contributing to a reserve or sinking fund on this basis.

You could of course compromise with a service charge cap, or by expressly excluding any planned big-ticket items. Note however that this may become a common problem as commercial leases are getting shorter and more flexible. On 6 July 2023, the Financial Times reported that: "The length of UK office leases has fallen to the lowest level on record while vacancies rates have soared close to a decade high [...]. Average lease lengths dropped to two years and 10 months in the first quarter, the lowest level since data was first collected in 2018, according to commercial property management platform Re-Leased."[25] (This fact, by the way, also highlights the importance of the stickiness driver for landlord's take-up of green leases, where they help generally to encourage a tenant's longer-term commitment to a property.)

25 Quinio, July 2023.

### 4.5.2 Mutuality

***How important is mutuality when it comes to sustainability provisions?***

At a multi-let building or estate, a tenant will clearly require a landlord to ensure all the other tenants sign up to broadly the same service charge provisions for consistency of expectation and cost recovery. Also consider mutuality from the point of view of the standards the landlord and the tenants will be held to when it comes to the use of sustainable materials, or cleaning products in the common parts and in each tenanted space for example.

Similar circular economy principles on the use of goods and materials in the common parts can also be incorporated via the tenant covenant on alternations and yield up, for example.

This ensures that the entire building or estate is managed and operated in a way that supports overarching targets, and this makes it easier to accept.

### 4.5.3 Asset specific considerations

***What special features of my building/estate can impact on the sustainability provisions in a service charge clause?***

It is really important to think practically about how tenant reasonable expectations of common parts can be undermined by well-intentioned sustainability provisions in service charge items. Where an estate includes landscaped areas, for example, aesthetics are likely to be key to a tenant's experience of occupation, and even the value of its brand. Clarify then how the Landlord's obligations around landscaping and maintenance will manifest in practice, to avoid later concerns around rewilding initiatives, or even signing up to "No Mow May".

### 4.5.4 Defining the service charge items

***How broad can the service charge items relating to sustainability be?***

At any given property, the scope for a landlord to assist in meeting environmental performance targets is likely to be broadest when a service charge is encourages expenditure on common parts. There is likely to be some debate however whether certain items or energy efficiency improvement works should bc covered as service charge items in the first place. Where the measure is expensive (and relatively infrequent), the parties may agree to a reserve or sinking fund to spread the cost over time (and between benefiting tenants).

But exactly what that might be included is very asset dependent. TCLP drafting is useful however, since it asks the tenant to prioritise supporting all environmental recovery. Going back again to Hannah's Clause, the definition of "Service Costs" is therefore supplemented to include "*Costs related to the gathering and processing of information relating to [Environmental Performance]*", and the concept of "Service", to be provided by the landlord, and for which costs will be recovered, includes:

> *"**Services**" – Implementing such measures, facilities or services as the Landlord considers appropriate to improve [Environmental Performance] including:*
>
> *a. installing separate [Service Media], metering and other appropriate monitoring equipment to capture data relating to the use, operation and occupation of the [Property] and/or the [Building] by tenants and occupiers for the purpose of assessing [Environmental Performance];*
>
> *b. installing new or additional motion or daylight controlled sensors and energy efficient bulbs or luminaries in the*

*[Retained Parts] [where, in the reasonable opinion of the [Landlord], such installation is likely to improve [Environmental Performance]];*

c. *carrying out inspections for the purposes of:*

   (i) *identifying any water leaks at intervals determined by the [Landlord] acting reasonably; and*

   (ii) *taking such steps as the [Landlord] considers appropriate to reduce water wastage [(including installing plant and equipment for the purposes of recycling water (including [Greywater]) and capturing and using rainwater)];*

d. *installing [such] facilities in connection with waste management [as the [Landlord] may from time to time consider appropriate, including for the purposes of compacting, recycling, composing, storing and disposing of refuse with a view to improving [Environmental Performance][in accordance with the [Waste Management Plan][;][; and]*

e. *[performing any of the [Services] in such a manner or by such methods as the [Landlord] may from time to time consider reasonably required to:*

   (i) *improve [Environmental Performance]; or*

   (ii) *avoid any adverse effect on the [Environmental Performance] of the [Property] and/or the [Building] or any [Adverse Climate Effect][; and*

f. *[in relation to any obligation to maintain gardens] where the [Landlord] considers it appropriate, introducing measures to promote [Biodiversity] in relation to maintaining gardens at the [Premises]].*

***How much extra will my client be expected to pay for environmentally friendly service charge items?***

Sourcing the kind of sustainable materials and procurement mechanisms promoted in Hannah's Clause might well cost more. The drafting even anticipates it. But how much is too much?

Hannah's clause prioritises environmental performance above cost liability in all circumstances, but does suggest excluding: "*the costs of improving, replacing or upgrading any item, plant or equipment [...] which is in good working order or is capable of economic repair at reasonable cost unless the [Landlord] (acting reasonably) considers that such improvement, replacement or upgrade is likely to result in an improvement in [Environmental Performance] or a reduction of the [Service Costs] associated with the consumption of energy or other resources.*"

Acting for a tenant however, you might want to consider again a service charge cap on contributions, or specific exclusions by way of compromise (such as those related to the costs of benchmarking environmental performance, or MEES regulations, which would ordinarily fall squarely on the landlord's shoulders anyway).

***Will the court help interpret service charge clauses widely to include environmentally sustainable, if more expensive, options?***

Generally, in the event of a later dispute over what can and can't be deemed included within a service charge schedule, the courts will judge the drafting on the basis of the contra proferentem rule, i.e. against the draftsman. This effectively means that if it's not clear, it isn't covered.

Also, interestingly, there has been to date no help from the courts in importing sustainability clauses to an old service charge provision. In the context of a Landlord and Tenant Act 1954 renewal, see Chapter 5, paragraph 5.4 for more information. It's not clear whether, on a contractual renewal when a tenant expects substantially the same terms, the courts might be more willing to impose additional service charge provisions like those considered here, however this does highlight the importance of clarity on that cost allocation upfront.

## 4.6 Recovery of costs via rent review

Parties which have already signed up to the common mechanism of a periodic open market rent review will need also to agree how energy improvement works carried out by, or paid for, by the tenant over the term of the lease will be treated on review.

This topic further complicates the dark art that rent review calculation can often seem to be. While overall, efforts to increase a building's environmental credentials may be rewarded in a green lease, works undertaken to improve an asset's performance and its efficiency in utilities use will normally reflect well in an open market rent review. Broadly then, rent review surveyors might assume that more hypothetical tenants are interested in renting it, and that the open market rent should increase as a result. What this means is that a tenant who has already paid for the actual works risks paying a second time via an increased rent.

So how should building works permitted (or required) by either landlord or tenant to improve the environmental credentials of a property, be treated on rent review?

This light green drafting comes from the BBP Green Leases Toolkit:

> *Rent Review Disregards – Any works carried out by the Tenant carries at its own expense, provided they are carried out in compliance with the lease, should be disregarded.*

Notes on this clause:

4.6.1 Dovetailing rent review with liability for works in the lease

***What happens if the tenant has carried out energy improvements not because it had to, but because it wanted to?***

BBP's solution is to ensure that a tenant can broadly assume the works it carries out *at its own expense* to reduce utility bills or improve the building's performance will not be rentalised on review. On the other hand, of course, this disregard does not capture *every* possible category of energy improvement works. If the landlord pays for the works it seems fair, as BPP says in its Green Lease Toolkit that "*any benefit which such savings would have on the open market rental value of the Premises should be taken into account on review*".

But how possible is it in practice to identify improvement works that have been carried out by the landlord and the costs of which have already been covered via the service charge? Technically the drafting might not be enough to ensure that the tenant doesn't pay twice.

4.6.2 Drafting for rental impact outside a rent review mechanism

***What if the parties agree to amend the rental figure periodically, dependent on energy efficiency targets?***

A landlord can theoretically use rent levels to carrot and stick tenant adherence to energy efficiency targets, although there are good reasons to avoid this. Reducing the rent if targets are met is a compelling and no doubt attractive offer for tenants, but of course the landlord's own financing will likely be predicated on receiving that clear FRI income stream.

The flip side is a rachet upwards, if the tenant *fails* to meet specified energy reduction targets. Be aware of the tax traps on increasing rent outside the pre-agreed review mechanism. Very basically, if the rent increases within the first five years of a term, the tenant could find itself liable to an additional stamp duty land tax (SDLT) liability at the appropriate rate (see SDLTM13155 – Calculation of Stamp Duty Land Tax (SDLT): Rent: Variable or uncertain rent: Review of estimate).

## 4.7 Recovery of costs via yield up provisions

At the end of the term, standard leasing practice generally involves the tenant making good at the property: dismantling its alternations; removing its chattels; and giving back the property empty, ready to be handed over to the next tenant. If this reinstatement is not literally undertaken, it is paid for in a negotiated dilapidations settlement. In the context of environment performance targets however, this is inherently problematic. There are likely to be negative environmental consequences and waste generated by a tenant having to reinstate, and no guarantee it is not entirely wasted effort in any case if the landlord subsequently knocks the building down or the incoming tenant has extensive fit out plans.

The following examples of drafting each achieve a similar green effect at the end of the term:

The BBP Green Lease Toolkit offers a compromise solution to ensure that, at the end of the term, a landlord requiring reinstatement will first have to *consider* avoiding the need for destruction where this will have an adverse impact on the building's environmental performance:

> *The Tenant shall not be required to reinstate any tenant's alterations which have been carried out lawfully during the term where such reinstatement would adversely affect the Environmental Performance of the Premises or the Building unless such reinstatement is reasonably required by the Landlord having regard to its intentions in respect of the use or re-letting of the Premises or the Building after the expiry or sooner determination of the term.*

Aatmay's Clause from TCLP similarly starts from the principle that reinstatement is not necessary without good reason:

> *1. The [Tenant] shall not be required to reinstate any alterations carried out in accordance with this [Licence] where each of the following apply at the expiry or sooner determination of the [Term]:*
>
> *1.1 any such reinstatement is not reasonably required by the Landlord [not less than three months prior to the end of the Term having regard to the Landlord's intention in respect of the use or re-letting of the [Premises] [Property] [and/or Building]]; and*
>
> *1.2 any such reinstatement would [materially] adversely affect the [Environmental Performance] of the [Premises] [Property] [and/or Building] [and/or the EPC rating of the [Premises] [Property][and/or Building]].*

TCLP also offers Rosie's Clause, a good example of dark green drafting since to insist upon reinstatement, the landlord must explain its impact on reversionary value.

> *By the [End Date] the Tenant must have removed [INSERT DETAILS] save that the [Tenant] shall not be required to remove any [Environmental Improvements] [unless the [Landlord] has given the [Tenant] at least [NUMBER] months' notice that it requires the [Tenant] to remove all or part of any [Environmental Improvements] on the basis that those works remaining after the [End Date] would have a detrimental impact on the investment value of the [Landlord's] reversionary interest in the [Premises], [Building] or [Estate]].*

Notes on this clause:

4.7.1 Extent of landlord control

***Which party should be responsible for calculating and deciding whether to incur the environmental costs of reinstatement?***

The BBP drafting is certainly a chance to address wastefulness, albeit the final decision is entirely within the gift of the landlord. Commercial landlords are highly unlikely ever to skip on the opportunity to have the occupational tenant make good the space or pay at least for the damage. Exerting some control over this process is what makes the landlord confident they can fulfil their letting strategy and minimise vacancies while maximising income from the property.

## Theme 4 – Amendments to standard tenant covenants

Far and away the largest section of a commercial FRI lease is the tenant covenants: prohibitions, for the most part, on how the property will be occupied. Underlying each of these covenants will be the standard FRI principle that the landlord retains control over the capital value of the asset and its rental value. Anything that the tenant might do therefore on or to the land that jeopardises either is verboten.

In this context, it is interesting to see how green lease principles need not undermine this control. They can in fact maintain these values, and this is surely the narrative behind landlord and tenant adoption.

## 4.8 Alienation

Having gone to the tremendous effort to draft a green lease; establish the forum; and strategize on the processes and plans necessary to support and improve a property's or an estate's sustainability and environmental performance, a landlord could be nervous when the tenant comes for consent to an assignment or underlet. Unfettered alienation will leave the landlord having to deal with a new party, whose operational energy draw or technological engagement or brand identity could well be different. The light touch aspirations of co-operation should be threatened.

The NHS green lease suggests at the dark green end of the drafting spectrum that the landlord should: "*Consider whether Tenant is only permitted to assign/underlet to an organisation who can demonstrate good environmental sustainability credentials*".

Attempts to restrict the incoming party or undertenant on the basis of its environmental concerns are very much in their infancy. A tenant will be anxious to maintain its capacity for a fast(ish) exit and even though the landlord will clearly want its investment to date recognised in rental sums, it is easy to see how restrictive alienation drafting could actually negatively affect the rental levels it could achieve on open market review, by restricting the pool of willing tenants. Above all, setting acceptable credentials is fraught with difficulty.

## 4.9 Alterations (fit out)

At the outset of a leasing arrangement, an incoming tenant will usually be contemplating its fit out. These exercises are often carried out pursuant to a licence, entered into under an agreement for lease, rather than the lease itself, however the landlord will want its green lease provisions to dovetail neatly with environmental expectations at the outset.

Detailed technical specifications are routinely given by tenants for a fit out and depending on the scope, they might attract BREEAM compliance, net zero targets or circular economy principles.

This simple drafting came from the BBP Green Leases Toolkit.

> The [Tenant] shall procure that its [Fitting Out Works] comply fully with the following requirements of the [BREEAM New Construction Scheme] current at the date the works are carried out: *[set out in detail, preferably using the BREEAM credit reference, the elements of the work that the [Tenant] will be carrying out]*

Landlords and tenants may also be keen to reduce unnecessary waste on construction works, or the purchasing of new products (and the associated GHG emissions). In this case, they can follow circular economy principles such as those set out in Aatmay's Clause from TCLP, which is designed to fit within a licence for alterations (or fit out):

> *1. Carrying out and Completing the Works*
>
> *1.1 The Tenant must carry out and complete the Works (and ensure that the Works are carried out and completed): 1.1.1 using (to the extent reasonably practicable) good quality Materials that are fit for the purpose for which they will be used and to the reasonable satisfaction of the Landlord; 1.1.2 in accordance with a Waste Management Plan* and using [best/ [all] reasonable] endeavours to minimise Waste; 1.1.3 in accordance with Efficiency Standards to mitigate against any Adverse Climate Effect; and 1.1.4 at all times in a manner which maximises the prospect of achieving the Efficiency Objective on Practical Completion [and during the operating life] of the Works.*
>
> *1.2 For the purpose of assessing whether practical completion of the Works has been achieved, the [Employer/ Employer's Agent/ Architect/ Contract Administrator] shall not issue any certificate to that effect until such time as the EPC Obligation has been met.*
>
> *1.3 The failure of the Tenant to comply or procure compliance with the provisions of clause [1.1] will constitute a [substantial] breach of this Licence.*

Notes on this clause:

4.9.1 Using construction industry standards

***Is BREEAM an appropriate standard for the tenant to conform to with its fit out?***

Importing net zero or carbon standards on construction projects can all make a real difference. When a new property is built, the developer/owner will often aim to for a particular BREEAM "New Construction" rating, to increase marketability. This is generally beyond scope of leasing documentation, but the landlord will be keen to ensure that any"Good", "Excellent" or

"Outstanding" rating it has at the property is not compromised by a tenant's fit out. This can occur where the fit out encompasses elements of the building assessed as part of the rating (e.g. lighting, air conditioning, certain materials and building services).

An assessor tasked with allocating a BREEAM rating will consider the contractual obligations that control a Tenant's fit out works. These would usually be in a licence to alter, but possibly in an agreement for lease or the lease itself. Once these are in place, and an initial BREEAM "New Construction" rating has been awarded for the property generally, a rating cannot be prejudiced by the tenant's activity.

Consider then in the context of the fit out the stage of development of the property itself, and whether BREAM is too strict. You could refer to a more generic fit out guide.

*How do circular economy principles work?*

A circular economy provision prioritises the use of reclaimed, re-used or recycled goods or materials over new items. Where that is not possible, it calls for sustainable goods or materials to be chosen.

The definitions in Aatmay's Clause from TCLP are taken partially from the EU's Waste Framework Directive (2008/98/EC). Its accompanying definition of "Materials" sets out a hierarchical structure for how to minimise waste:

- ***Materials** means:*
  - *(a) Reused Materials or Reclaimed Materials, but where these are not available or appropriate then;*

(b) *Sustainable Materials, but where these are not available or appropriate then;*

(c) *Recycled Materials, but where these are not available or appropriate then;*

(d) *Recyclable Materials, but where these are not available or appropriate then;*

(e) *materials or products.*

- ***"Reused Materials"*** *means materials, products or components that are not waste and are used again for the same purpose for which they were conceived.*
- ***"Reclaimed Materials"*** *means materials that have been removed from another building or site, which can be reused in the [Premises][Property][and/or Building] without substantial modification.*
- ***"Sustainable Materials"*** *means products or materials:*

  a) *which are extracted, produced and made in a way that minimises the Embedded Carbon;*

  b) *which are extracted, produced and made without depleting non-renewable resources and without disrupting the established steady-state equilibrium of the environment and key natural resource systems; and*

  c) *which are recyclable or reusable*
- ***"Recycled Materials"*** *means materials which, through a recovery operation, have been reprocessed into products, materials or substances whether for the original or other purposes.*
- ***"Recyclable Materials"*** *means materials which can go through a recovery operation by which waste materials are reprocessed into products, materials or substances whether for the original or other purposes.*

Note of course that this hierarchy requires a fair degree of hands on control and inspection, as well as product understanding. The average commercial landlord is unlikely to be an expert in this topic yet will need to be prepared to engage with the tenant on its choice of materials throughout the process. It could easily end up becoming onerous for each party. And what happens if the materials used are not as defined? More consideration on the enforcement point is at paragraphs 4.23 to 4.26.

*Any other materials questions on materials to consider?*

A landlord might want to prevent certain products such as tropical wood from being used in fit outs. Standards are for example set in the EU with the European Union Timber Regulation (EU) No 995/2010 (on the trade of timber connected to deforestation and forest degradation) and its Conflict Minerals Regulation (EU) 2017/821 (which controls minerals often linked to armed-conflicts and related human rights abuses). While these are not directly relevant to the UK since Brexit they are useful for understanding and definitions in the event the landlord wants to control the existence of various problematic materials.

## 4.10 Alterations (general)

Alterations to a property rarely start and stop with the tenant's fit out. During the term of the lease, the tenant may require any number of modifications or alterations so that the property continues to suits its occupation. These will almost certainly be controlled by an alterations covenant of the lease, with works authorised by a licence to alter.

It is already common that this clause prohibits any mooted alternations out of the gate where they jeopardise the existing EPC (standard) rating or, more broadly, the energy performance of the building. But what else can be asked of an alteration covenant? The answer is quite a lot as it happens.

The MCL simply places an onus on the tenant to consider the impact of its works:

> *The [Tenant] will take into consideration any impact on the [Environmental Performance] of the [Premises] from any proposed works to or at the [Premises].*

The NHS Green Clauses meanwhile doesn't just prohibit any alterations to the property or its plant that adversely affect Environmental Performance or an EPC; it also drafts for a subtly different new approach. In this example, the starting position is that the tenant *can,* with consent, carry out non-structural alterations designed to improve Environmental Performance provided they don't adversely impact other services:

> *1. The [Tenant] may, with the [Landlord's] consent (which shall not be unreasonably withheld) carry out alterations to the [Property] which are designed to improve the [Environmental Performance] of the [Property] and/or the [Building], provided that such alterations:*
>
> *1.1 will not adversely affect the performance or the life cycle of any mechanical or electrical services, or any other plant, equipment or services in the [Building]; and*
>
> *1.2 are not structural alterations.*

Notes on this clause:

### 4.10.1 Landlord control

***What freedom should a tenant have to carry out works that increase Environmental Performance?***

The NHS clause clearly controls the tenant's freedom to carry out works as it retains the overarching requirement for landlord consent. This could however be subject to the standard modification "not to be unreasonably withheld or delayed", and what constitutes reasonable could even be understood in the context of an overall environmental impact.

## 4.11 Use

Commercial leases commonly control the use of the property. As well as being clear on a "specific permitted user" definition, restrictions will prevent prohibited uses. Traditionally, these have referred to intangible categories such as "immoral" use, which tended to veer towards preventing the (legal) sale of pornography or racy underwear, so that certain retail chains have been refused access. It will be interesting however to see if use covenants will ultimately be used by the landlord to control uses that may adversely affect the energy performance of the property. Subjective concepts Immorality lasted decades; this is arguably much easier to interpret and evidence.

## 4.12 Use of energy and utilities

Beyond mutual energy performance targets to save energy and CO2-emissions, leasing parties rarely address the sources of electricity supplied to a building at the outset of lease negotiations. It is possible however to commit to procuring a renewable energy supply that will virtually overnight reduce the building's carbon footprint and the parties' scope 3 emissions, and aid the achievement of net zero goals.

Lotta's Clause from TCLP provides the following drafting, with obligations for both landlord and tenant, as a starting point for the lease parties to consider ensuring a supply of green electricity to property:

> *1. Landlord's Obligations – Electricity Supply*
>
> *1.1 The [Landlord] shall procure electricity for the [Premises] that is 100% [Renewable Energy].*
>
> *1.2 The [Landlord] shall provide the [Tenant] on demand with appropriate documentation to evidence the energy sources used to generate electricity for the [Premises].*
>
> *2. Tenant's Obligations – Electricity Supply*
>
> *2.1 If the [Tenant] procures any electricity for the [Premises], it shall be 100% [Renewable Energy].*
>
> *2.2 The [Tenant] shall provide the [Landlord] on demand with appropriate documentation to evidence the energy sources used to generate any electricity procured by the [Tenant].*

Notes on this clause:

4.12.1 General complications

***Isn't renewable energy more expensive?***

In short, yes. There will likely be a financial burden for selecting greener energy sources. But this can be alleviated with bulk discounts or, depending on the scope of ambition for onsite renewables, the ability to sell energy back to the grid.

Bear in mind though that tenants do actually already have a right to request under the Electricity and Gas (Internal Markets) Regulations 2011 that their electricity comes from another supplier. Also note that any clauses dealing with the provision and cost of utilities should anticipate the impact of taxes such as the Climate Change Levy (a tax on energy delivered to non-domestic users, designed to incentivise increased efficiency).

*What about a multi-tenanted building or estate?*

This covenant is drafted as an absolute requirement. Clearly this can be difficult on a multi-tenanted building or estate unless *all* the parties agree to the requirement, the additional costs and the installation of any necessary equipment, potentially within let demises. Alternatively, the landlord can take control of all energy provided in order to select a particular energy provider, then pass it through to occupational tenants. Bulk energy rates might then be available to offset some of the higher costs, and act as a selling point to tenants.

In fact, especially on estates, landlords appear to be moving in an 'energy flexible' direction. Onsite, technology and renewables can reduce costs in the common parts, and energy from photovoltaic panels, for example, can be sold back to the grid. This involves understanding the landlord's current and future energy management plan, in order to draft for the flexibility to adopt and install new green technology for example. You may need to assess the rights and reservations (see paragraph 4.14), to ensure the landlord will be able to carry out its plans.

### 4.12.2 The difficulties of definitions

***What is renewable energy anyway?***

Defining renewable energy gets technical very quickly, but TCLP suggests the following definitions for use in Lotta's Clause:

- ***"100% Renewable Energy"*** *means an energy system where all the energy used is sourced from Renewable Energy Sources.*
- ***"Renewable Energy Sources"*** *means naturally replenishing non-fossil sources of energy, including but not limited to hydropower and tidal power, hydrothermal power, aerothermal power and geothermal power, wind, and solar which are in each case eligible for certification by REGO Certificates.*
- ***"REGO Certificate"*** *means a Renewable Energy Guarantees of Origin [or an equivalent] certificate for all energy consumed within the Premises and generated from a recognised source of renewable energy for which such certificates are available.*

(Note that when using this definition of "**Renewable Energy Sources**", you could specifically exclude the incineration of regenerative biomasses (things like municipal waste and biodiesel) since this production process emits significant quantities of GHG/small particulate air pollution. Naturally replenishing sources of energy might be preferable.)

***How can a leasing party identify renewable energy suppliers?***

It's worth also noting that this obligation can be surprisingly complicated to achieve. In the UK, electricity purchased from the wholesale transmission grid will come from all sources, including fossil fuels. This means that a UK energy supplier cannot generally control the source of its electricity without procuring it 'directly' from green generators or generating the power itself in wind or solar farms. Suppliers can "match" energy for green tariff consumers with energy generated from renewable sources (as evidenced by traceable Renewable Energy Guarantees of Origin (REGO) certificates). The parties may need to ask questions to ensure compliance

## Theme 5 – Amendments to Landlord rights and reservations

Of course, particularly in a multi-let building or an estate, it won't just be the tenant making alterations. Landlords work on the common parts, and they are likely to require the ability to access a tenant's demise to carry out their own ad hoc works to increase environmental performance; or follow through on a sustainability plan; or install green equipment such as charging stations for electric vehicles or solar systems on roofs. They may just want to access metres to track energy consumption and obtain reports. In the absence of these specifically drafted rights however, landlords could find their hands ties, and be forced to wait for void periods between leases to carry out works.

### 4.13 Access rights

A simple access right is contained in the BBP Green Leases Toolkit:

> 1. *The Landlord and/or its agents may (on giving reasonable prior notice to the Tenant) enter and remain on the Premises (with workmen, contractors and necessary equipment) at reasonable times for any of the following purposes:*
>
>    a) *taking reasonable steps to review or measure the Tenant's energy and water use and its waste production or waste management save where up-to-date information in this*

> *respect has already been provided to the Landlord by the Tenant*
>
> *b) carrying out [at the Landlord's expense] works [which are agreed by the Tenant (acting reasonably) and are] intended to improve the Environmental Performance of the Building (provided that such works cause as little disruption as reasonably possible and when complete do not adversely affect the Tenant's beneficial use and occupation of the Premises)*
>
> *2. The Landlord shall make good [at its own expense], promptly and in a good and workmanlike manner, any damage caused to the Premises by the carrying out of such works.*

Notes on this clause:

4.13.1 MEES exemptions

***Will a broadly drafted access right jeopardise the ability of the landlord to claim an exemption under regulation 31 of MEES?***

A common reason for landlord entry is, sensibly, for any necessary inspection for the production of an EPC. Where the drafting also permits works to be undertaken however, it could impact on the landlord's MEES strategy. As discussed in Chapter 2, paragraph 2.3.2, the exemption in regulation 31 speaks to any third-party consent required for works to be carried out, so that the landlord need not comply with MEES where a necessary third-party consent is not forthcoming.

It's very risky leaving this out on purpose. Of course, the absence of a wide enough access right is not necessarily sufficient proof for the exemption. And in order to benefit from it, the landlord must still use "reasonable efforts" to obtain tenant consent (and a tenant could always welcome entry for energy efficiency works even where it is not a given). Besides, there could well be additional third-party consent hurdles, such as listed building consent, planning permission or mortgagee approval.

## 4.14 Rights to carry out works

Once in the tenant's demise, the landlord will need separate rights to actually carry out relevant works relating to energy efficiency Such a reservation/right will necessarily be property specific but may well need to be sufficiently broad to be future proof as technology and EPC ratings change. The BBP Green Leases Toolkit contains:

> *[The Landlord shall be entitled to carry out works to the Common Parts and the plant and equipment serving the Building, which are intended to improve the Environmental Performance of the Building notwithstanding any interruption in the provision of services by the Landlord provided always that the Landlord shall use reasonable endeavours to minimise any disruption to the Tenant and any interference with services it has covenanted to provide].*

Drafting from Hannah's Clause from TCLP is meanwhile helpful with thinking about the categories of green technology and equipment a landlord might ultimately want to install:

> *A landlord may install:*
>
> - *"separate service media, metering and other appropriate monitoring equipment to capture data relating to the use, operation and occupation of the Property and/or the Building by tenants and occupiers for the purpose of assessing environmental performance;*

> *- new or additional motion or daylight controlled sensors and energy efficient bulbs or luminaries in the Retained Parts [where, in the reasonable opinion of the Landlord, such installation is likely to improve environmental performance]"*

The NHS green lease clauses also refer to categories of green measuring equipment, the type useful for metering and data collection (see paragraph 4.3):

> *The Landlord may at its own cost install equipment (whether fiscal meters, sub-meters or check meters or other equipment) to measure the supply of gas, electricity or other energy or utility supplied to the Property and the Landlord and/or its agents shall have the right to enter and remain on the Property (with workmen, contractors, and necessary equipment) at reasonable times in order to carry out such works*

In the meantime, placing constraints on the works a Landlord can undertake in the common parts or in respect of plant and machinery is unusual, but this can be done to avoid an adverse environmental impact (effectively a reciprocal restriction to the tenant's alteration covenant in paragraph 4.11).

This drafting also comes from the BBP Green Leases Toolkit. The suggestion of seeking tenant consent is relatively light green in its effect, but on the whole this clause is unlikely to be a problem for a tenant provided there are no cost consequences (such as via service charge):

> *The Landlord shall not carry out any works to the Building or to the plant, equipment or services within and serving the Building which [may/will] adversely affect the Environmental Performance of and/or any EPC rating of the Premises and/or the Building*

> *[unless it first obtains the [written] consent of the Tenant to such works [such consent not to be unreasonably withheld or delayed]].*

## Theme 6 – Additional new tenant covenants

Sector, asset, corporate and geographic-dependent, ESG is an exceptionally broad concept. So far, all the green lease clauses discussed in detail in this chapter have spoken to the E, or green, limb of ESG. There are ideas however, or examples of drafting, that respond to initiatives taking place on properties which directly develop an assets' or an asset owner's social (S) or governance (G) credentials.

The market is at the very start of a journey to incorporate these points. It may well be asking too much of a standard leasing arrangement, but attention in this area seems likely to increase. Leases are not the natural home for enforcing corporate board diversity targets, for example, but there may be opportunities where operational strategy directly touches the land. Provisions that meet corporate social and governance targets can be drafted therefore, although templating is clearly difficult. The exact objectives and the scope of the parties to agree on them, will necessarily be very asset specific, and very much dependent on the set up at the property.

In no particular order then, you could consider drafting for the following examples of initiatives that touch on every ESG limb:

### 4.15 Drafting for detailed operational directions

A building handbook or manual is likely the right place in most situations involving detailed policies and general directions (such as to switch lights off, use energy efficient light fittings, or recycle), albeit that general tenant compliance is then also covenanted for.

Many of these policies can address S or G initiatives. It is worth knowing for example that a category within the GREB scoresheet called "Management and consumption" looks for attempts at energy management; water management; waste management; indoor environmental quality management; sustainable procurement; sustainable utilities; sustainable transport; and sustainable cleaning practices. Much of this might sit within a building management plan or manual if not the lease itself.

Similarly, it could also be made clear in the handbook that the tenant entity is expected to ensure its employees undertake training to ensure initiatives on energy use or waste disposal are properly implemented.

## 4.16 Drafting for sustainable travel to and from the property

Where the landlord has a sustainable travel plan for an estate, and wants to curate a holistic environmental experience for tenants, it might consider lease clauses that *require* tenants to support its sustainable travel plan. Perhaps they will need to provide employees or visitors with shower facilities or bike racks, or cover the cost of such installations via the service charge.

While expectations may be set out in a lease or building manual, note that Raphael's Climate Change Due Diligence Procurement Questionnaire, a Supplier Questionnaire from TCLP, asks potential suppliers at question 30: "*Does the Supplier have any policies in place to reduce the environmental footprint caused by travel/commuting?*" Green lease drafting becomes then an exercise in thinking broadly about how the client's contractual, operational relationships interact.

## 4.17 Drafting for sustainable procurement

Commercial buildings rely on an astonishing number of services to run efficiently and seamlessly for the business taking place within their walls. Services like catering and cleaning play a vital role, and their component parts are key to a business' supply chain. This is another area which has not historically been impacted by the terms of a lease, however a landlord might want to ensure sustainable practices are bedded in to a supply chain or products used on site are chosen for their sustainable credentials.

The category "Management and consumption" within the GRESB scoresheet asks for details on sustainable cleaning practices, for example. And Aatmay's Clause from TCLP uses the following definition to frame product choice:

> ***Sustainable Procurement*** *means the purchase of products or materials (including packaging) which are extracted, produced and made:*
>
> - *without depleting non-renewable resources (including without limitation any Finite Power Source);*
> - *without disrupting the established steady-state equilibrium of the environment and key natural resource systems; and*
> - *which are reusable and recyclable.*

Raphael's Climate Change Due Diligence Procurement Questionnaire, a Supplier Questionnaire from TCLP, meanwhile asks potential suppliers to provide information on a wide range of climate change-related issues and this operational detail can certainly be picked up in a building handbook. Consider question "*17. […] what, if any, steps have been taken to […] use recycled goods/packaging where possible, […], to use local, low GHG emissions materials and labour, to implement circular economy and zero waste principles, to give surplus materials to community projects [...]".*

## 4.18 Drafting to ensure efficient plant

Where the premises contain plant and equipment, there is a useful overarching covenant in the NHS Green Clauses suite:

| *[Tenant]/[Landlord] to keep plant/ equipment in efficient working order.* |
|---|

## 4.19 Drafting to reduce reliance on single use plastics

Particularly where a site has a staff canteen, Alice's Clause from TCLP is a great example of how lease drafting can maximise the impact of initiatives on relatively granular change. This controls the availability of single use plastics on site:

> *1. The [Parties] shall assess and identify the volume by weight [and/or other measurements] of [Single Use Plastics] in the provision of the [Services] [and/or [Supplies]] ...].*
>
> *2. The [Service Provider] shall provide the [Employer] with a [monthly/quarterly/annual] service report within [five (5) days] [of the end of each [Measurement Period]] indicating the then current volumes by weight [and/or other measurement] of [Single Use Plastic] used in the [Services].*
>
> *3 The [Service Provider] shall reduce the volume of [Single Use Plastics] used [...]*
>
> *1.5 If the [Service Provider] fails [...] then:*

> *(a) this shall be deemed a [Service Failure]; and*
>
> *(b) a [Service Payment Deduction] shall be made by the [Employer]. [...]*

## 4.20 Drafting for social issues in a retail park or shopping centre

Thinking particularly about a retail context, such as a shopping centre or retail park, there are various operational requirements a landlord might want to invoke to ensure the property as a whole operates sustainably and with strong social credentials, attracting consumer footfall as well as brands.

Given the need to engage retail competitors in this exercise, it might well be important that mutual confidentiality, such as that in the shared forum drafting discussed at paragraph 4.2, provides the safe space to discuss social initiatives, particularly when they impact different retailers differently. Tenants might be generally prevented from stocking or advertising certain goods, like real fur, or from destroying unsold products as waste. This is a risk where luxury fashion brands want to avoid unsold stock being sold off cheaply and undermining the brand,[26] but less likely to be contentious for a stationer.

## 4.21 Drafting for Governance issues

Drafting for the G limb of ESG is especially difficult (neither landlord or tenant will welcome third party interference in its internal corporate processes) but at its simplest level, a lease

26 When Burberry came under fire in 2018 for this practice, its defence that "energy generated from burning its goods was captured" was unconvincing. Kollewe, 2018

agreement will likely already require general tenant compliance with applicable laws and regulations.

This obligation could of course be mutual. And drafting could be clear that this will include laws relating to corruption, competition, privacy, product and consumer safety, and occupational health and safety.

Consider however how compliance could ever be monitored, as neither landlord nor tenant can assume responsibility in practice for checking general legislative compliance, Perhaps it will simply be the case that when, for example, Tesco (other high profile national supermarket brands are available), breaches competition law, a landlord will want to reserve the right to forfeit the brand from its portfolio? What about if a tenant breaches a commitment to pay employees the London Living Wage however? Drafting here will require significant and detailed commitments from all the leasing parties.

## Theme 7 – Remedies and enforcement on breach

The elephant in the room when it comes to any of the green lease clauses discussed in this chapter is enforcement. What, ultimately, happens if the tenant (or the landlord, as the case may be) fails to adhere to the new green lease obligations?

The fact remains that many green lease clauses are actually extremely hard to enforce, particularly where they depend purposefully on vague notions of co-operation or the use of endeavours (see paragraph 4.1.1). Even where obligations are clear, establishing breach is likely to be cost-and labour-intensive, and rely in any case on the landlord being tipped off to its potential.

So, is there in practice any scope to invoke the standard remedies for new green lease breaches?

## 4.22 Forfeiture

Forfeiture is generally the nuclear end game for every landlord. A forfeiture clause will usually enable a landlord to recover the property on non-payment of rent or other material sums, or following breach of material covenant, or even a material breach of any covenant. Of course, the immediate consequence of the landlord is the ending of the rental stream, but also as an equitable remedy it is always subject to the tenant's application to the court for relief. And depending on the breach, the court could always find that the tenant's failure was not considerable enough to warrant the draconian removal of its business premises.

It remains to be seen then, whether forfeiture will be the resolution needed to deal with landlord frustrations over tenant failures to adhere to green lease drafting. In any case, the relative importance of the green lease covenants (their materiality) will undoubtedly be entirely dependent on things like the landlord's public environmental commitments. Does it really matter if the tenant fails to disclose data, for example, essential to the landlord's corporate reporting or benchmarking requirements? What if it fails to turn the lights off?

## 4.23 Self-help remedies

Where the breach relates to physical condition of the property, the landlord may be able to side step forfeiture and rely on a "self-help" using the standard Jervis v Harris clause in a commercial lease.

This clause will permit the landlord to enter the demise to inspect the state of repair; to serve notice identifying defects; and then to carry out any work required where it hasn't already been carried out despite contractual obligations in the lease. Depending on the wording of the green lease then, such work might extend to fixing alterations that had an adverse effect on the EPC rating, for example, or to maintaining a meter or other data monitoring equipment, or to ensuring plant is efficient.

The main advantages to the landlord of using this clause will be that it avoids the need to try and forfeit, and that it controls the work throughout. Also, while the landlord will foot the bill for the remedial work in the first instance, it will be able to recover the costs as they are reclaimed as a debt. Of course, the landlord will need to be careful to avoid accusations of trespass or attract a restraining injunction, but in practice this remedy first and foremost highlights the need for clarity in the green lease obligations.

## 4.24 Damages

Even assuming that a clear breach of the green lease clause is evident, assessing the extent of financial damage is foreseeably challenging, not least because the success of most clauses depends on the standard of environmental efficiency at the property. And even where the loss can be linked to the breach, it is still subject to the standard mitigation requirements.

## 4.25 New remedies

The sanctions for new green lease provisions on breach are not entirely clear, but it might be worth thinking less about the stick, and more about a carrot.

Clauses relying on an underlying pledge of co-operation set the scene for an approach that focuses on aligned corporate objectives. Landlord and tenant could use those early Environmental Forum meetings to define clear Key Performance

Indicators (KPIs) that incentivise both parties. And tenant activity may be easier to channel into environmental strategies where it involves minimal or no change to its standard practice. Landlords can meanwhile only market a building that already contains the correct meters or measuring equipment, for example.

By working together at the outset of a lease negotiation, and setting clear and realistic expectations for this brave new world of leasing, the parties can give the drafting the best chance of making a considerable difference.

# CHAPTER FIVE

# SEEKING OTHER OPPORTUNITIES TO IMPORT GREEN LEASE PROVISIONS

We have seen how much of green lease drafting involves a new focus on landlords and tenants engaging and co-operating to achieve sustainable goals, whether in relation to a building's operation, or in order to meet their own corporate goals. It may well be however that the hardest part of any negotiation is identifying and agreeing on the genuine opportunities to bring the parties to the table.

Of course, it's not always possible to draft a green lease from scratch. Where leasing arrangements are ongoing, landlord or tenant clients hoping to benefit from green provisions will have to wait for a break in the term to renegotiate clauses. As part of an ongoing client relationship therefore, real estate lawyers will often diarise key points in the lifetime of a leasing arrangement, ready to remind clients for example about upcoming breaks, terminations, or rights of renewal. In this way, they are also well placed to identify opportunities to incorporate green lease drafting or principles into a letting.

This chapter considers when those opportunities might arise during an on ongoing letting, and the likely scope of a landlord or tenant (as they case maybe) to be able to introduce new sustainability ideas or targets at such a time.

## 5.1 The need for deeds of variation

Clearly, any attempt to introduce new binding tenant obligations via a side letter or building management plan during the course of an existing lease term is likely to be largely ineffective when it comes to binding obligations. A side letter could of course be countersigned by the recipient tenant, however this will not be enough to vary the terms of a registered lease.

The tenant will clearly need to formally agree to taking on additional responsibility, and due to the complexities of the issues involved, the safest approach is using a formal deed of variation where the ongoing lease is created by deed. Common law long dictated that deeds could only be varied using a deed, to avoid relying on equity, and this is particularly important where you are importing new obligations on the tenant, for example to cover the cost of energy efficiency obligations, or to engage formally with the landlord on the process of commissioning an EPC. A deed of variation also enables you to deal holistically with green issues as they touch upon various clauses in the lease (for example Chapter 4, paragraph 4.4), but remember to ensure any guarantor is looped into any extended liability (*Holme v Brunskill (1877) 3 Q.B.D.*) to avoid compromising a security package.

The challenge clearly comes in a multi-tenanted building or estate, where the landlord will want to import substantially similar obligations across its entire property simultaneously, so that any EPC or sustainability strategy can be properly implemented, managed or planned. part is particularly important if such a strategy is at the request of, or with the support of, a financing party or shareholders. In this scenario, the roll out of the plan will have to be realistic and well managed.

This said, if the intention is merely to introduce aspirational wording to act co-operatively or consider shared goals, you could actually find it simpler (and cheaper) to acknowledge the difficulties in creating biding obligations and enter into a Memorandum of Understanding.

## 5.2 Using a Memorandum of Understanding

In many ways, the informality of this approach is its strength. A memorandum of understanding in this context is a document akin to a side letter. It will be signed by both landlord and tenant but it won't actually vary the terms of an existing lease with formal covenants. It isn't, technically, legally binding.

Nonetheless, by containing language in which the parties agree "to work together" or "give reasonable consideration to [...]", it can set out a useful framework of policy intentions; a roadmap for the co-operation required to actually improve the environmental performance of a property. In so doing, it can help each party fulfil its environmental aspirations.

It might not be enough to ensure absolute tenant compliance with a formal ESG or sustainability strategy, but there is something to be said for the fact that a memorandum of understanding is a nimble tool. It can be drafted at any stage. It is easily updated or replaced. And it does provide a starter for ten in charting shared ambitious, expected divisions in responsibility for environmental initiatives, and creating clarity on the incentives for the parties to make change. As discussed in Chapter 3, paragraph 3.3.2, this approach is at the vanguard of a cultural shift for FRI leasing. Better still, these documents are not registrable at the Land Registry and so remain confidential as between the parties.

In terms of generating the drafting, a template memorandum of understanding can be found as part of the BBP Toolkit. There is also one in the NHS Green Clauses suite, where it has been supplemented by some additional wording. Both are short documents. Short and sweet, and largely uncontroversial for both parties involved.

## 5.3 Building Management Handbooks, etc

For completeness, of course it's not inconceivable that a landlord, particularly in a multi-tenanted building or on an estate, produces a handbook for tenants that speaks directly to day-to-day operations. It might include user manuals for equipment, and details on the management of recycling etc. The tenant will generally be required to occupy the property and operate in accordance with this, although tenant adherence is likely to be via a clause which requires the tenant to comply "to the extent it does not conflict with the terms of the lease".

These kinds of documents are created and maintained by landlords, but a proactive landlord can certainly lead by example in the industry with apply similar sustainable operational or equipment obligations to its activities in the common parts.

In practice then, while this kind of handbook might help ensuring that equipment is operated in a certain (efficient) way, or that certain categories of recycling are routinely sorted and collected, any attempt to implement a broader ESG strategies or import new covenants of the type detailed in Chapter 4 will likely be ultimately unenforceable if they are left in this handbook.

## 5.4 Renewal lease negotiation in the context of 1954 Act

When leases protected by security of tenure under the Landlord and Tenant Act 1954 (the 1954 Act) come to the end of their contractual term, the tenant may well hold over in the premises while parties embark on negotiations to create a new lease of the same space. Such new leases are usually based on the old ones, however the case law to date has placed some interesting considerations around attempts at redrafting to incorporate new green provisions.

A new lease granted in the context of 54 Act renewal is often a good opportunity to introduce some necessary updating. Protected leases tend to be granted for longer contractual terms in the first place, and so will often come to the negotiating table with some outdated legislative or statutory references. It's not uncommon in practice then that either landlord or tenant will spot the welcome opportunity for updating the drafting, all in knowledge that the courts can step in in the event that the parties cannot agree between themselves.

***So what scope is there for introducing green lease clauses into 54 Act renewal leases?***

To date, as the concepts of green leasing gain traction in the commercial market, we must assume that the majority of attempts to incorporate green drafting into 1954 Act renewal leases have gone unreported. Perhaps this is because in the context of an ongoing letting relationship, neither party has yet used the Landlord and Tenant Act 1954 renewal mechanism to import green lease drafting wholesale; perhaps the parties were aligned on change; perhaps the changes proposed were not actually contentious as between the parties, specifically or generally.

Attempts by landlords to incorporate amendments that seek to control or mitigate the draconian consequences of MEES regulation have, at first instance, fared less well however. In November 2020, during a four-day hearing. the country court considered renewal terms after a newsagent and stationer's unopposed section 26 application for a new shop lease in the Westfield Centre, Shepherd's Bush. The result, in *W.H. Smith Retail Holdings Limited v Commerz Real Investmentgesellschaft*

*MBH (17-20 November 2020, 25 March 2021)*, was a stark reminder of the court's restricted ability to intervene.

When the landlord argued that its attempt to import new sustainability-related service charge provisions (such as energy efficiency improvement works, environmental audits, and implementing EPC recommendations) represented "reasonable modernisation as they reflect changes in law since the agreement for lease pursuant to which the existing lease was granted in November 2007", the court disagreed. The drafting was not clear; the obligations were the landlord's. On 25 March 2021, it found, inter alia, that it was not reasonable for the landlord to include additional liabilities in a statutory lease renewal. Parkes J, at paragraph 41, was clear. The landlord could not argue that vague sustainability modernisation was required and rely "on the uncertain mantra that everything will be conducted in accordance with the principles of good estate management."

Another good example was explored a year later at Sheffield County Court (*Clipper Logistics Plc v Scottish Equitable Plc (2022) Unreported, 7 March 2022*). Leeds-based retail logistics company Clipper Logistics Plc had been renting an industrial unit in Rotherham. Its lease expired in September 2020 however its occupation was protected by the 1954 Act and so Clipper embarked on negotiations with its landlord Scottish Equitable Plc for a new lease. Not unusually, Scottish Equitable saw an opportunity to drop in various new updater clauses into the draft, however when the parties could not agree, it was for the County Court to determine its exact contents.

In March 2022, the County Court heard that the points of contention all effectively stemmed from attempts to import some of the green lease provisions we have considered in Chapter 4, Specifically, Scottish Equitable wanted new tenant covenants to:

- **prohibit** the tenant from carrying out alterations that would leave the property with a lower than band E EPC rating (i.e. that would render the property "sub-standard" under the existing MEES regulations, and which could leave the landlord liable for the penalties discussed in Chapter 2, paragraph 2.3.1);

- **indemnify** the landlord for the costs of commissioning a new EPC where alterations had been made by the tenant or any other occupier; and

- **return/reinstate** the property at the end of the lease term with the same EPC rating it had a lease grant, having carried out any necessary remedial works to restore the EPC rating if it had fallen.

The onus would clearly fall on Scottish Equitable to persuade the judge that the terms of the existing tenancy should be changed, and that the changes themselves were fair and reasonable as between the landlord and the tenant (*O'May v City of London Real Property Company Limited [1983] AC 726*). The changes needed ultimately to constitute a reasonable stab at modernisation.

These amendments do not arguably seem unreasonable or unfair at first glance. There is clearly a reasonable justification for a landlord drafting to avoid finding itself in breach of MEES. And it is not, on the face of it, unfair to require a tenant to recover an EPC rating lost on its own watch. Nonetheless, the court returned to one overarching principle in MEES when giving its judgment. It found that MEES is first and foremost a *landlord* responsibility, and no reasonable modification would shift the burden of its compliance onto a tenant. It is for the landlord to let a standard rated building.

With this lens, the court could see clearly that the effect of Scottish Equitable's amendments, when taken together, would be to hand over to the tenant the legal duties and responsibilities that belonged solely to the landlord under MEES. This shift of liability was de facto unfair and unreasonable, providing an unfair advantage for the landlord and unreasonably burdening the tenant, and the court was therefore able to find that:

- **on the prohibition** – this amendment was not reasonable since it was unnecessary. The form of lease the parties were renewing already contained a tenant covenant effectively prohibiting and controlling alterations to the property;

- **on the indemnity** – this amendment was not reasonable since it placed a cost burden (potentially significant) on the tenant; and

- **on the reinstatement provision** – it was reasonable for the landlord to protect itself against tenant inaction, and it could therefore require that the tenant return the property at the end of the lease with the same EPC rating it had had on day one of the term.

It's not clear of course whether, were parties to find themselves in court arguing about the terms of a contractual renewal (as opposed to a 1954 Act renewal) which anticipated substantially the same terms, the courts could be willing to introduce stricter green lease provisions. For the time being however, for at least some of the green lease provisions discussed in Chapter 4, the message from the lower courts is that they will judge in accordance with a key principle of MEES: the bulk of the obligations fall on, and will remain squarely on, the landlord.

Of course, in practice, this means that the onus is on the landlord and its lawyers to incorporate future proof green leasing at the outset of a new letting which is to be protected by the 1954 Act.

Where MEES wasn't foreseeable or drafting impossible, the onus is now on negotiation after the service of a section 26 notice, to frame drafting changes in the context of broader considerations.

# CHAPTER SIX

# THE ROLE OF THE REAL ESTATE LAWYER

Having considered the commercial and environmental rationale for, and contents of, green leases, it is worth a moment to consider the role the real estate lawyer can play in this brave new world. We advise on and facilitate the full gamut of real estate transactions. But to what extent *must* lawyers equip themselves with relevant knowledge about climate change, and be prepared to introduce and recommend ideas to clients that might be only the smallest part of the solution for global, social problems, despite these being far beyond the scope of the initial, traditional instruction?

## 6.1 The Law Society and climate conscious legal practice

There is little doubt that to offer credible and authentic advice on green leases and market shifts in the context of the climate emergency, real estate practitioners will need to think more broadly about the motivations of their clients and the operational impact of their property assets than perhaps ever before. We operate within a highly regulated industry however, and it's fair then to ask to what extent this professional stretch can or must be made.

There has been no formal regulatory guidance as yet from the Solicitor's Regulation Authority (SRA) to explain what exactly lawyers in England and Wales *have to* do with regard to considering the impact of climate change. Our main body of representation, The Law Society of England and Wales, has nonetheless stepped recently into what was fast becoming a lacuna in professional guidance, and offered a compelling glimpse of a likely professional direction.

On 19 April 2023, the Law Society published its long-awaited milestone guidance note: "The impact of climate change on solicitors", in which it clearly placed our practices, our existing professional duties to clients, and ultimately the scope of every one of our instructions, within an expanded context that involved understanding and advising on climate legal risks. This note actually followed the body's own Climate Change resolution in October 2021, when it promised to "*provide guidance to solicitors on how, when approaching any matter arising in the course of legal practice, to take into account the lately impact of that matter upon the climate crisis in a way which is compatible with their professional duties and the administration of justice*".

This, in turn, was an unprecedented step for the Law Society, but cannot have been a huge surprise to commentators. Its promise to "develop plans and take rapid action, in a manner which is consistent with restricting global warming to 1.5°C, by adopting science-based targets", was not exactly leading the climate change combatting charge of the professional services sector. It had merely picked up the baton against the climate crisis, from the many professional bodies that had already done something similar. Just in the real estate world, for example, the Royal Institute of Chartered Surveyors (RICS), the Chartered Institute of Architectural Technologists (CIAT) and the Chartered Association of Building Engineers are among many who had already signed the Professional Bodies Climate Action Charter.

Still, it is hard to overestimate the importance of the 2023 milestone note. The detailed 28 pages of guidance was a huge step for every solicitor in England and Wales. Regardless of the particular field in which they practice, it frames the start of new modus operandi for the whole legal world. In the event of any accusation of negligence for a future failure to advise on climate risks, the note is "likely to be afforded considerable weight by the courts" (Tromans KC's opinion, paragraph 30). And its conclusion was very clear: "solicitors, always in a way which is compatible with their professional duties and the administration of justice, [should] engage in climate conscious legal practice."

## 6.2 The April 2023 milestone guidance note

The milestone guidance note covers an extraordinary amount of ground as it seeks to map this new world. It is split into two broad sections:

- **Part A** considers the governance and ethics of law firms operating in a climate change context, providing high-level information to help them design and implement their own climate-conscious corporate strategy; and

- **Part B** provides more detailed analysis of the kind of risks we face with client change, and the interplay between these, the provision of legal advice and the scope of solicitors' professional duties.

### 6.2.1 Running a climate conscious law firm?

The note opens with a section to help law firms design and implement their own corporate strategy for climate change.

Many law firms are already setting targets to reduce their own organisational climate impact, and these will undoubtedly vary dramatically in scope, ambition, and time frame. With the best will in the world, a sole practitioner is unlikely at this stage to have had the time and space to create and publish a fully-fledged Net Zero Strategy. Still, for any organisation making public statements or commitments, or releasing reporting against those targets, it can be difficult in a climate conscious environment. As well as the SRA's Standards and Regulations, law firms are governed by the Competition and Markets Authority's guidance on environmental claims (Green Claims Code), which ensures public statements are accurate and not misleading.

We have also already seen in Chapter 2 how audited reporting obligations may be mandatory, depending on a law firm's size, or even adopted voluntarily, but firms risk being guilty of greenwashing if their marketing or pitch materials ultimately mischaracterise or overstate their targets, or progress made against them. Clear and consistent language is necessarily then at the heart of any goal or target setting. Given the complexities of the use and application of various climate change concepts therefore, the Law Society is keen to ensure everyone is on the same page. Part A therefore discusses the role of science-based targets in relation to dealing with the GHG emissions produced by each law firm.

Emissions may effectively be quantified in scope buckets – calculated in terms of whether they were generated from fossil fuel combustion on site (scope 1), via the purchase of electricity, heat or steam from a third party (scope 2), generated by a supply chain (scope 3) or associated with advisory operations (scope 4, or advised emissions). The language develops constantly but the principles are key. By operating and advising on matters in certain sectors, especially those which can attract heightened scrutiny, law firms are at particular risk of being judged against their advised emissions. It is clearly important then to understand how these can arise in an organisational or corporate context, and appreciate the risk that they are used as a proxy for judging whether the relevant law firm is, in fact, as committed to reducing emissions or climate change mitigation as it says.

In terms of practice management, the note also reminds us that firms are communicating their climate ambitions not just to (potential) clients, but also to (potential) employees. The employment market has been challenging since the Covid 19 pandemic and, in that respect, law firms might share concerns with clients (Chapter 3). Many observers suggest that this *war for talent* is increasingly, often significantly, influenced by an employer's approach to climate change. The law Society suggests this also requires some consideration in the context of guidance from the Employment Appeals Tribunal (EAT): could the definition of a recognised 'philosophical belief' as a protected characteristic under the Equality Act 2010 extend to a commitment to climate change?

Of course, in the context of this book, the majority of law firms are also tenants of and consumers of commercial property. It will be interesting then to see then how many are incentivised by the existence of the milestone note to find opportunities to green their own leases. Getting their own houses in order is fundamental to offering that informed and authentic advice to clients.

### 6.2.2 The expanding scope of solicitor's duties?

The day-to-day practice of every solicitor in the country is framed by SRA principles and duties, those fundamental tenets of ethical behaviour. We learn them at law school, but they are not set in stone; the practical interpretation of these has always evolved over time. Sir Thomas Lund, the former secretary general of the Law Society, is quoted in Part B as saying in 1960: "Global social issues interact with these solicitors' regulatory duties and the way the regulator enforces those duties." Admittedly, he was not referring specifically to the impact of climate change, but the principle can easily be applied to today's climate challenge.

Part B of the milestone guidance therefore pays particular attention to how four key solicitors' duties could well develop in response to the climate emergency:

#### 6.2.2.1 Duty to exercise reasonable care and skill

Up first is the general legal **duty to exercise reasonable care and skill**, to the standard of a reasonably competent practitioner (*Midland Bank Trust Co Ltd v Hett Stubbs and Kemp [1979] Ch 384*). In practice, this already means that a real estate solicitor must be aware that they may, at any time, have to look beyond the narrow scope of an instruction. In time, it could mean assessing whether, and to what extent, climate legal risks are relevant on the leasing transaction. Perhaps there will be embedded in the results of practical transaction diligence, such as flood searches, or perhaps green lease drafting can anticipate the costs of improvements ultimately necessitated by those risks.

#### 6.2.2.2 Duty to warn

We are also expected as solicitors to be able to warn clients about potential risks in a transaction, specifically by pointing out hazards of a kind which should be obvious to the solicitor but which the client may not appreciate (*County Personnel (Employment Agency) v Alan R Pulver & Co [1987] 1 WLR 916*).

As the Law Society points out, this "should be addressed by a solicitor at all stages of your advice" and can already extend to information obtained while fulfilling the retainer, which may not be expressly within its scope (*Minkin v Landsberg [2015] EWCA Civ 1152; [2016] 1 WLR 1489*). Back to our green lease context, this could well mean considering the character/experience of the client, to assess whether they may or may not need advice or information or warnings that are reasonably incidental to the retainer. There's no easy answer here, particularly given the varying resources of our clients, but has a commercial client made its own net zero commitments and/or public commitments to climate change? Do they have sophisticated or specialist knowledge in this area?

#### 6.2.2.3 Duty to disclose

Solicitors must always disclose to their client all information material to the matter at hand, of which they have actual knowledge.

In the context of climate change however, this is particularly interesting. Few citizens could now claim to have *no* knowledge of climate change, but misinformation and misunderstanding is rife. And a natural extension of this duty is in understanding *how* any relevant risks are disclosed. The Law Society is firm ("disclose these in a clear and understandable way") but we are not climate scientists. Explaining any risk in this context will clearly involve developing new understanding and skill.

#### 6.2.2.4 Duty to uphold service and competence levels

This duty comes hand in hand with the former one. Continuing competence is a fundamental tenant of lawyering. Responsibility falls on practitioners to consider training needs as part of their professional development. Accordingly, the SRA Code of Conduct for Solicitors (SCCS) and the Code of Conduct for Firms (SCCF) require that "the service you provide to clients is competent and delivered in a timely manner" and that it takes account clients' attributes, needs and circumstances.

At first glance, this is an existing regulatory duty to develop as the job demands. The problem for a legal profession in a climate change context however is in balancing the potential failure to upskill quickly enough in this area against reputational damage and a breakdown in client relationships. Failing to mention climate risks is not necessarily a regulatory breach *yet*, but the problem is a chicken and egg one. As solicitors undertake climate change training, widespread awareness and acknowledgement of climate issues will only grow. And this will in turn likely intensify the expectation over time that a reasonably competent solicitor is able to analyse the impact and relevance of physical and transitional climate change risks to a transaction.

Of course, we will never be climate science experts, but neither are we experts in flood risk or invasive weeds and yet sub-heads on search results or Japanese Knotweed often appear in our property reports… Of course, this often involves signposting specialist third-party assistance when it is likely needed.

## 6.3 How can you respond to the potential for extended regulated duties?

Assuming our regulated practice follows in the direction the Law Society anticipates, lawyers will need to understand how to deal effectively with the evolved duties, especially when they cannot draft or negotiate the client's way out of the risk. There are a number of strategies to consider:

### 6.3.1 Train and develop relevant expertise?

A real estate lawyer cannot become a climate expert overnight; indeed, they couldn't realistically be expected to become experts in this technical and scientific discipline over the course of an entire legal career. However that is not what the Law Society is suggesting. Without being a bona fide expert, a practitioner can still be trained to identify and anticipate particular pinch points that might commonly arise in real estate, especially in the transition risk areas of regulation and legislation.

This might mean, for example, drawing the dots on likely future asset insurance costs when the flooding risk of the property remains high after the Flood Re scheme ends in 2039. It is also likely to mean, as the January 2023 *Green leases and Minimum Energy Efficiency Standards* guidance published by the Law Society already concluded, that solicitors acting on lease transactions should be able to discuss the implications of MEES. In the context of this book, it must surely also mean that we are aware of the development and demand for green leases, and be prepared to consider their application as transactions land on our desks.

When it comes to getting training in and understanding physical climate risks and their impact on property assets, it is worth reiterating that real estate practitioners are already well versed in identifying these, albeit without necessarily explaining the climate wrapper. As discussed in paragraph 6.2.2.4, we have been including analysis of physical risk such as flooding, for example, in standard reporting on purchases and fundings for a long time. We're not experts in the cultivation and eradication of Japanese Knotweed, but we raise requisitions and report to the client. We signpost experts for involvement where necessary. We flag the potential for tax risk. We do, routinely, stretch our service further than the initial transaction scope.

### 6.3.2 Undertake extended DD on property transactions?

Extended due diligence feels like an inevitable consequence of any conclusion on extended duties, and the search industry has been waiting ready in the wings, developing new products focused on presenting climate risks as they affect individual property assets.

Clearly this field is nascent, and continually changing. At the time of writing, possibly the most prominent offer has been created by property search provider Groundsure, which took the bold step of commissioning a legal opinion in July 2022 on the issue of expanding regulatory duties, from eminent environmental law expert Stephen Tromans KC. His overarching opinion was clear at paragraph 68(9): "My view is that an experienced conveyancer should be aware of physical and transition climate risks and should as part of their retainer take steps to warn their client about them and advise on steps to respond to that risk." In this way, Groundsure's ClimateIndex™ product, which uses forward climate scenario modelling to establish the risk of climate change, is able to market itself as clearly "supporting your compliance with the Law Society Guidance on Climate Risks including duty of care and duty to warn."

Of course, at the time of writing, other climate related searches are also available. Landmark Information Group produces specific residential and commercial climate searches, for example, as well as offering a Climate Change Portfolio Assessment and its RiskHorizon platform, an ESG management tool. Theoretically, right now, any of these commercial searches could satisfy Tromans KC, who says at paragraph 68(11) of his legal opinion: "An obvious step is to make use of the commercial search tools which are available." There is a residual problem here for legal practitioners however, since the task of selecting between the searches on offer is a complex one. Underlying data sources differ, as do the exact menu of climate risks focused on (which might include physical coastal erosion or wildfires, for example, or transition risks in the form of EPC data). There will have to be a decision on which search, for any individual property, is the most appropriate.

Moreover, "the conveyancer's duty extends not only to undertaking such searches for the client but also communicating the results and their implications to the client." (Tromans KC's opinion, at paragraph 68(11)). Helpfully then, when it comes to dealing with the climate changes searches in the context of a standard report on title, Marni's Clause from TCLP provides two drafting options, for the situation in which a client either instructs a solicitor to carry out a climate search (Option A) or does not (Option B).

Option A effectively appends the search result, summarises its conclusions while making it abundantly clear that "*we are not qualified to advise on the results of the climate search*" and then, importantly, sets out a series of *what next* recommendations. It is now that legal advisers can highlight the other professionals and specialists that might be needed to assess and quantify transition risks (most obviously valuers and insurance brokers) or physical risks (such as surveyors or structural engineers). In the alternative, Option B ensures that "*the consequences of the client's decision to not commission the climate search shall be borne by the client alone*".

It will be interesting to watch this market develop over time, and close attention will need to be paid to prevent ordering a search being nothing more than a tick box in a transaction.

### 6.3.3 Exclude climate issues from your retainer?

A retainer, or engagement letter, should be produced for the client at the start of every transaction. It can usually, of course, be limited by written agreement and indeed retainers routinely exclude areas of legal advice that the relevant lawyer is not providing comment on, such as tax. If, for at least the foreseeable future, lawyers are conscious then that they are simply not competent to advise on climate risks at all, or even to direct the client to an appropriate professional, can they also exclude climate change issues from the scope of the retainer?

Theoretically the answer is yes, but there is a bit of a legal lacuna, since informed consent is generally required to exclusions from the retainer. This means a practitioner *could* find themselves having to explain rather circuitously the significance of the relevant risk issue that they are hoping to not actually advising upon. In this situation, "the care and effort likely to be required by the solicitor [...] seem to me likely to make that a very unattractive course" (Tromans KC's opinion, at paragraph 45).

This point has not been tested in court however and so in the meantime, the risks that remain to be seen are really whether attempts to carve out climate legal risks would have negative competitive and/or reputational consequences, particularly when so many law firms are publicising their climate commitments and credentials.

### 6.3.4 Insure against advising on climate legal risks?

There is undoubtedly work to be done here on the response of the insurance industry to both professional indemnity and asset insurance in the context of climate risks. Like the rest of us, insurers are increasingly aware of climate issues, and solicitors will need to be well versed in current/prospective PII requirements if they are to ensure affordable future cover. For the time being, it is probably best to assume there will ultimately be a query on professional indemnity renewal to explain how solicitors are increasing their competence on climate change issues.

## 6.4 What next for guidance and regulation on this topic?

We are still waiting for the SRA to set out its official regulatory position on these matters but would be wise to anticipate formal advice from the legal industry regulator in the foreseeable future. In the meantime, the Law Society's milestone guidance from April 2023 was necessarily broad in its application to legal practice, catering for lawyers across all practice areas and sectors, across the whole of England and Wales.

Admittedly it does make a start on analysing the vast smorgasbord of potential risks caused by climate change, and an appendix helps with understanding and articulating these. The next step however is honing tailored practice area advice with the production of far more detailed practice notes, each setting out clear instructions and breaking down the Law Society's expectations in a practical way for practitioners.

At the time of writing, the Law Society is at the start of a process of consultation on the form of such a practice note for the property world, which will ultimately be aimed at both commercial and residential real estate lawyers.

> *"Lawyers thrive in change, their job depends on it. Although the risks climate change presents to both planet and people are unprecedented in our times, this will not be the first nor last time lawyers have had to adapt to change. In fact it presents an opportunity to enhance client advice in a manner which both protects them and the planet."*
>
> – Alasdair Cameron, Policy Adviser: Climate change and Planning and Environmental Law, The Law Society

# CHAPTER SEVEN

# CONCLUSION – THE FUTURE IS GREEN

Change is coming.

There's no silver bullet to counter the effects of the climate crisis, but as part of a multi-faceted approach to an incredibly complex problem, green leases undoubtedly have an important role to play.

A nascent green lease tool is emerging from the gloom. While the UK government procrastinates over serious top down legislative and policy solutions to the climate emergency, landlord clients are already building a brave new world from the bottom up. It almost doesn't matter if MEES will ultimately tighten standards within the decade, or whether new operational efficiency ratings will be mandated. The commercial real estate sector has already been busy redefining what it means to create truly sustainable bricks and mortar. Demands might be made for recycled construction materials, or renewable energy supplies, but sustainability might also now mean nurturing and protecting the humans that work within and around it.

Until green leases find their institutionally-accepted market standard, each incarnation will be the unique and complex product of a clients' particular goals and aspirations, melded with an assets' physical reality. Chapter 3 runs through a number of fantastic and freely available drafting tools that can be borrowed and manipulated. This new generation of green leasing may have started with documenting rather limited aspirations of strict regulatory compliance, but it will, and is already, taking on considerable sophistication. All born from the fact that clients are willing to put their money where their mouth is on sustainability, and they will reap the benefits that follow.

As lawyers then, we stand at the vanguard of a rapidly developing service profession, with an important task. We must talk about green leases, but we must also listen to our clients. We have a role to educate on the drafting possibilities, but also to properly understand the practical commercial elements and operational realities of environmental strategies. These things have, realistically, been long outside our wheelhouse. But just as definitions of environmental performance may need to be tailored to embed realistic macro and micro targets; so 'new' climate risks and demands need to be catered for in our contracts: both physical and transitional. By truly understanding the scope of this task, and by framing the possibilities clearly, real estate practitioners are therefore crucial to supporting the commercial real estate sector as it gets its own house(s) in order.

And as we partner with commercial clients, so our drafting has the power to change behaviour with immediate, lasting and measurable impact. In a way that supports multi-faceted climate change mitigation which, with everything crossed, has some hope of keeping us in line for a future based on the more acceptable range of RCP, and preventing widescale economic and social catastrophe.

The fact is that green leases are a real opportunity. We can carry the message to the market that it is possible to manipulate established FRI norms without losing commercial control or jeopardising the capital or rental value of investments. There is considerable evidence that aligning landlord and tenant interests is not motherhood and apple pie, but it is now a valuable commercial strategy to drive value by cementing commitments to future-proofed assets. And in what has to be one of the most positive outcomes from the resultant shift in FRI principles, we can all flourish in an environment of collaboration and creativity. Leasing need not be adversarial; it can be the product of shared goals.

The road to a truly sustainable standard green lease is not exactly without potholes, but this journey is one we must make together, sharing learning and experience along the way.

Like most real estate lawyers, I spend hours in the real world pointing at buildings and boring my children with reminiscences about the time I once worked on the contractual documents behind their past development, or their previous anchor letting or their historic covenants. It's fun (for me) but it would be infinitely better to leave the past behind, and to tell a tale of what might be expected for their exciting new futures.

# BIBLIOGRAPHY

Websites


- **Better Buildings Partnership (BBP) Green Lease Toolkit** – https://www.betterbuildingspartnership.co.uk/green-lease-toolkit

- **BREEAM** – https://bregroup.com/products/breeam/

- **The City of London Law Society Land Law Committee Certificate of Title (Eighth Edition 2023) and Note to Users** – file:///C:/Users/Intel%20NUC/Downloads/CLLS-Certificate-of-title-Eighth-Edition-2023-and-Note-to-Users.pdf

- **Green Lease Leaders (GLL)** – https://www.greenleaseleaders.com/green-lease-library

- **Global Real Estate Sustainability Benchmark (GRESB)** – https://www.gresb.com/nl-en/

- **Green Claims Code** – https://greenclaims.campaign.gov.uk/

- **Groundsure** – https://www.groundsure.com

- **Institute for Market Transformation** – https://www.imt.org/resources/green-lease-language-examples/

- **Landmark** – https://www.landmark.co.uk/geodata-services/environmental/

- **Law Society** – https://www.lawsociety.org.uk/topics/climate-change/

- **Model Commercial Lease** – https://modelcommerciallease.co.uk/
- **NABERS** – https://www.nabers.gov.au/publications/energy-efficiency-commercial-buildings
- **NHS model green lease for commercial premises** - https://www.england.nhs.uk/publication/model-form-green-lease-clauses-template/
- **Professional Bodies Climate Action Charter**– https://professionalsclimatecharter.org/
- **PRS Exemptions Register – Non-Domestic Register (EPC)** – https://www.ndepcregister.com
- **RED Foundation** – https://www.theredfoundation.org/
- **Royal Institution of Chartered Surveyors' (RICS) – Service Charges In Commercial Property (1st Edition)** – https://www.rics.org/profession-standards/rics-standards-and-guidance/sector-standards/real-estate-standards/service-charges-in-commercial-property-1st-edition
- **Solicitors' Regulation Authority (SRA) – Code of Conduct for Solicitors** – https://www.sra.org.uk/solicitors/standards-regulations/code-conduct-solicitors/
- **Solicitors' Regulation Authority (SRA) – Code of Conduct for Firms** – https://www.sra.org.uk/solicitors/standards-regulations/code-conduct-firms/
- **TCFD** – https://www.fsb-tcfd.org/
- **The Chancery Lane Project** – https://chancerylaneproject.org/

## Books, Publications and Articles


- Akila Quinio. Alex, **UK office leases shorten and vacancies rates soar as workers stay at home**, Financial Times, 6 July 2023. https://www.ft.com/content/5cc8ae2e-765c-43be-9f84-9426408e9609

- BBP. **BBP responds to changes in Government climate change policy**, 22 September 2023. https://www.betterbuildingspartnership.co.uk/bbp-responds-changes-government-climate-change-policy

- BEIS, **Final Stage Impact Assessment for the Private Rented Sector Regulations**, 2014. https://www.gov.uk/government/consultations/private-rented-sector-energyefficiency-regulations-domestic

- Climate Change Committee, **Progress in reducing UK emissions – 2023 Report to Parliament**, 28 June 2023. https://www.theccc.org.uk/publication/2023-progress-report-to-parliament/

- Green Building Council, **The Whole Life Carbon Roadmap – Answering your data FAQs received to date**, 26 April 2022. https://ukgbc.org/news/the-whole-life-carbon-roadmap-answering-your-data-faqs-received-to-date/

- Guardian staff and agency. **Monday was hottest day for global average temperature on record, as climate crisis bites.** The Guardian. 4 July 2023: https://www.theguardian.com/world/2023/jul/04/Monday-was-hottest-day-for-global-average-temperature-on-record-as-climate-crisis-bites

- Haggerty, Maryann. **Change is Coming: Climate-Risk Disclosures and the Future of Real Estate Investment Decision-Making, Urban Land Institute**, 14 September 2023. https://knowledge.uli.org/reports/research-reports/2022/climate-data-mandates-and-real-estate-investment-decisions?_gl=1*1rg17py*_ga*MTg5OTQ4NzczMy4xNjk1OTMwOTc3*_ga_68JJQP7N7N*MTY5NTkzMDk3Ni4xLjAuMTY5NTkzMDk3Ni4wLjAuMA

- Hansard, **Debate on the Minimum Energy Performance of Buildings Bill**, Volume 730, 24 March 2023 https://hansard.parliament.uk/Commons/2023-03-24/debates/6CBD1CB0-7EF6-4F82-BAE6-0BA219153E47/MinimumEnergyPerformanceOfBuildingsBill

- Harvey, Fiona. **Labour to stand firm on net zero policies and attack cost of Tory retreat.** The Guardian, 25 September 2023. https://www.theguardian.com/environment/2023/sep/25/labour-to-stand-firm-on-net-zero-policies-and-attack-cost-of-tory-retreat

- Hausfather, Zeke. **Focus on carbon offsets; UK expands oil and gas; IEA's path to 1.5C unpacked.** DeBriefed, 29 September 2023. https://www.carbonbrief.org/debriefed-29-september-2023-focus-on-carbon-offsets-uk-expands-oil-and-gas-ieas-path-to-1-5c-unpacked/

- HMRC internal manual, **Stamp Duty Land Tax Manual**, 19 March 2016, including **SDLTM13155 – Calculation of Stamp Duty Land Tax (SDLT).** https://www.gov.uk/hmrc-internal-manuals/stamp-duty-land-tax-manual/sdltm13155#:~:text=Once%20the%20end%20of%20the,after%20the%20five%20year%20period

- IFRS, **IFRS Foundation welcomes culmination of TCFD work and transfer of TCFD monitoring responsibilities to ISSB from 2024**, 10 July 2023. https://www.ifrs.org/news-and-events/news/2023/07/foundation-welcomes-tcfd-responsibilities-from-2024/

- IPCC, 2000: **IPCC Special Report on Emissions Scenarios.** Prepared by Working Group III of the Intergovernmental Panel on Climate Change. Cambridge University Press, Cambridge, United Kingdom, and New York, NY, USA.

- JLL, **Decarbonizing the Built Environment**, 20 June 2021. https://www.jll.co.uk/en/trends-and-insights/research/decarbonizing-the-built-environment

- Kollewe, Julia, **Burberry to stop burning unsold items after green criticism,** The Guardian, 6 September 2018. https://www.theguardian.com/business/2018/sep/06/burberry-to-stop-burning-unsold-items-fur-after-green-criticism

- Laville, Sandra. **'Pathetic': what scientists and green groups think of UK's net zero U-turn,** The Guardian, 20 September 2023. https://www.theguardian.com/environment/2023/sep/20/scientists-and-green-groups-dismay-at-uks-net-zero-u-turn

- Law Society. **Green leases and Minimum Energy Efficiency Standards Guide,** 20 January 2023. https://www.lawsociety.org.uk/topics/climate-change/green-leases-and-minimum-energy-efficiency-standards

- Legal Futures. **Non-compliance with energy efficiency standards could cost commercial property sector over £1 billion in annual rental income.** 22 September 2023. https://www.legalfutures.co.uk/associate-news/non-compliance-with-energy-efficiency-standards-could-cost-commercial-property-sector-over-1-billion-in-annual-rental-income

- Met Office, **Future weather forecast for the year 2050**, July 2020. https://www.metoffice.gov.uk/services/insights/future-weather-forecast-for-2050

- Met Office et al. **UKCP18 Guidance: Representative Concentration Pathways,** Met Office Hadley Centre, Environment Agency, Department for Environment, Food and Rural Affairs, and the Department for Business, Energy and Industrial Strategy, 2018. https://www.metoffice.gov.uk/binaries/content/assets/metofficegovuk/pdf/research/ukcp/ukcp18-guidance---representative-concentration-pathways.pdf (accessed 21 September 2023).

- NABERS. **NABERS UK to seek new administrator as BRE moves to focus on BREEAM**, 4 September 2023. https://bregroup.com/press-releases/nabers-uk-to-seek-new-administrator-as-bre-moves-to-focus-on-breeam/#:~:text=NABERS-,NABERS%20UK%20to%20seek%20new%20administrator%20as%20BRE%20moves%20to,its%20world%2Dleading%20BREEAM%20scheme

- Pickard. Jim, George Parker, Rachel Millard, Peter Campbell and Attracta Mooney. **What Sunak's net zero pivot means for UK climate goals and the next election,** Financial Times, 20 September 2023. https://www.ft.com/content/d44e70d1-19b7-4181-9267-5e38030d3d58?fbclid=IwAR1g9hH7HuJoI5zAy6k6bEbEt2njwnsVNTVuZL1ozMv47y_9BVXpqxWU9pY_aem_AQ7WtpCy7HleFILuFITcBOeoMJKPhD57nXGvgisjXtOhH7Xa7kU21JBbeifYrDhLBdzFI7k8dDtGn0YuV_emxlU8&segmentID=ba5c37f3-1ef2-1603-ca72-c26f292ab7db

- Smeeton. George. **Delaying insulation standards could cost private renters £1.4bn.** Energy and Climate Intelligence Unit. July 2023. https://eciu.net/media/press-releases/2023/delaying-insulation-standards-could-cost-private-renters-1-4bn July 2023

- Solnit, Rebecca. **Big oil coined 'carbon footprints' to blame us for their greed. Keep them on the hook.** The Guardian. 23 August 2021. https://www.theguardian.com/commentisfree/2021/aug/23/big-oil-coined-carbon-footprints-to-blame-us-for-their-greed-keep-them-on-the-hook

- TCFD, **Task Force on Climate-related Financial Disclosures 2023 Status Report**, October 2023. https://www.fsb.org/wp-content/uploads/P121023-2.pdf

- TCFD. **Final Report Recommendations of the Task Force on Climate-related Financial Disclosures**, June 2017. FINAL-2017-TCFD-Report.pdf (bbhub.io)

- Tromans QC. Stephen. **Advice in the matter of Conveyancers' Duty of Care to Advise Clients about Climate Risk and How to Discharge Such Duty**. 21 July 2022.

- Urban Land Institute, **Mapping ESG: A landscape review of certifications, reporting frameworks and practices**, May 2023. https://knowledge.uli.org/-/media/files/research-reports/2023/uli_esg_mapping-report_final---may-2023.pdf?rev=2e7eb61f072947f9a1ae9729406718f4&hash=BC3555839EECDB08B2465550E88A4BF4

- World Economic Forum, **Global Risks Report2022**, 11 January 2022: https://www.weforum.org/reports/global-risks-report-2022/

## Legislation

- **Business Protection from Misleading Marketing Regulations 2008 –** https://www.legislation.gov.uk/uksi/2008/1276/contents/made

- **Climate Change Act 2008 –** https://www.legislation.gov.uk/ukpga/2008/27/contents . 9 August 2023

- **Climate Change Act Target Amendment 2019 –** The Climate Change Act 2008 (2050 Target Amendment) Order 2019 (S.I. 2019/1056)

- **Company Act 2006 –** https://www.legislation.gov.uk/ukpga/2006/46/contents

- **Competition Act 1998 –** https://www.legislation.gov.uk/ukpga/1998/41/contents

- **Consumer Protection from Unfair Trading Regulations 2008 –** https://www.legislation.gov.uk/uksi/2008/1277/contents/made

- **Digital Markets, Competition and Consumers Bill 2023 –** https://bills.parliament.uk/bills/3453

- **Data Protection Act 2018 –** https://www.legislation.gov.uk/ukpga/2018/12/contents/enacted

- **Electricity and Gas (Internal Markets) Regulations 2011 –** https://www.legislation.gov.uk/uksi/2011/2704/contents/made

- **The Energy Performance of Buildings (England and Wales) Regulations 2012 –** https://www.legislation.gov.uk/uksi/2012/3118/contents/made

- **The Energy Efficiency (Private Rented Property) (England and Wales) Regulations 2015** (MEES) https://www.legislation.gov.uk/uksi/2015/962/contents/made

- **The Housing and Planning Act 2016** – https://www.legislation.gov.uk/ukpga/2016/22/contents/enacted

- **Landlord and Tenant Act 1954** – https://www.legislation.gov.uk/ukpga/Eliz2/2-3/56/contents

- **Minimum Energy Performance of Buildings (No. 2) Bill** – https://publications.parliament.uk/pa/bills/cbill/58-02/0150/210150.pdf


**Government consultations and guidance notes**


- Department for Communities and Local Government, **A guide to energy performance certificates for the construction, sale and let of non-dwellings** December 2017. https://assets.publishing.service.gov.uk/government/uploads/system/uploads/attachment_data/file/666186/A_guide_to_energy_performance_certificates_for_the_construction_sale_and_let_of_non-dwellings.pdf

- Department for Energy Security and Net Zero and Department for Business, Energy & Industrial Strategy, **Non-domestic Private Rented Sector minimum energy efficiency standards: EPC B implementation**, 17 March 2021. https://www.gov.uk/government/consultations/non-domestic-private-rented-sector-minimum-energy-efficiency-standards-epc-b-implementation

- Department for Energy Security and Net Zero and Department for Business, Energy & Industrial Strategy, **Introducing a performance-based policy framework in large commercial and**

**industrial buildings**, 17 March 2021. https://www.gov.uk/government/consultations/introducing-a-performance-based-policy-framework-in-large-commercial-and-industrial-buildings

- Competition and Markets Authority – **Green agreements guidance: how competition law applies to environmental sustainability agreements**, CMA177, 12 October 2023. https://www.gov.uk/guidance/green-agreements-guidance-how-competition-law-applies-to-environmental-sustainability-agreements

- Financial Conduct Authority. **Sustainability Disclosure Requirements and Investment Labels regime. CP 22/20. 25 October 2022.** https://www.fca.org.uk/publications/consultation-papers/cp22-20-sustainability-disclosure-requirements-sdr-investment-labels

## Case law

- Clipper Logistics Plc v Scottish Equitable Plc (2022) Unreported, 7 March 2022

- County Personnel (Employment Agency) v Alan R Pulver & Co [1987] 1 WLR 916

- Holme v Brunskill (1877) 3 Q.B.D.

- Jervis v Harris [1995] EWCA Civ 9

- Midland Bank Trust Co Ltd v Hett Stubbs and Kemp [1979] Ch 384 at 403

- Minkin v Landsberg [2015] EWCA Civ 1152; [2016] 1 WLR 1489

- O'May v City of London Real Property Company Limited [1983] AC 726

- WH Smith Retail Holdings Limited v Commerz Real Invesmentgesellshaft MBH, 17-20 November 2020, 25 March 2021

# MORE BOOKS BY LAW BRIEF PUBLISHING

A selection of our other titles available now:-

| |
|---|
| 'A Practical Guide to Estate Administration and Crypto Assets' by Richard Marshall |
| 'A Practical Guide to Managing GDPR Data Subject Access Requests – Second Edition' by Patrick O'Kane |
| 'A Practical Guide to Parental Alienation in Private and Public Law Children Cases' by Sam King QC & Frankie Shama |
| 'Contested Heritage – Removing Art from Land and Historic Buildings' by Richard Harwood QC, Catherine Dobson, David Sawtell |
| 'The Limits of Separate Legal Personality: When Those Running a Company Can Be Held Personally Liable for Losses Caused to Third Parties Outside of the Company' by Dr Mike Wilkinson |
| 'A Practical Guide to Transgender Law' by Robin Moira White & Nicola Newbegin |
| 'A Practical Guide to 'Stranded Spouses' in Family Law' by Mani Singh Basi |
| 'A Practical Guide to Residential Freehold Conveyancing' by Lorraine Richardson |
| 'A Practical Guide to Pensions on Divorce for Lawyers' by Bryan Scant |
| 'A Practical Guide to Challenging Sham Marriage Allegations in Immigration Law' by Priya Solanki |
| 'A Practical Guide to Legal Rights in Scotland' by Sarah-Jane Macdonald |
| 'A Practical Guide to New Build Conveyancing' by Paul Sams & Rebecca East |
| 'A Practical Guide to Defending Barristers in Disciplinary Cases' by Marc Beaumont |
| 'A Practical Guide to Inherited Wealth on Divorce' by Hayley Trim |
| 'A Practical Guide to Practice Direction 12J and Domestic Abuse in Private Law Children Proceedings' by Rebecca Cross & Malvika Jaganmohan |
| 'A Practical Guide to Confiscation and Restraint' by Narita Bahra QC, John Carl Townsend, David Winch |
| 'A Practical Guide to the Law of Forests in Scotland' by Philip Buchan |
| 'A Practical Guide to Health and Medical Cases in Immigration Law' by Rebecca Chapman & Miranda Butler |

| ‘A Practical Guide to Bad Character Evidence for Criminal Practitioners by Aparna Rao |
|---|
| ‘A Practical Guide to Extradition Law post-Brexit’ by Myles Grandison et al |
| ‘A Practical Guide to Hoarding and Mental Health for Housing Lawyers’ by Rachel Coyle |
| ‘A Practical Guide to Psychiatric Claims in Personal Injury – 2nd Edition’ by Liam Ryan |
| ‘Stephens on Contractual Indemnities’ by Richard Stephens |
| ‘A Practical Guide to the EU Succession Regulation’ by Richard Frimston |
| ‘A Practical Guide to Solicitor and Client Costs – 2nd Edition’ by Robin Dunne |
| ‘Constructive Dismissal – Practice Pointers and Principles’ by Benjimin Burgher |
| ‘A Practical Guide to Religion and Belief Discrimination Claims in the Workplace’ by Kashif Ali |
| ‘A Practical Guide to the Law of Medical Treatment Decisions’ by Ben Troke |
| ‘Fundamental Dishonesty and QOCS in Personal Injury Proceedings: Law and Practice’ by Jake Rowley |
| ‘A Practical Guide to the Law in Relation to School Exclusions’ by Charlotte Hadfield & Alice de Coverley |
| ‘A Practical Guide to Divorce for the Silver Separators’ by Karin Walker |
| ‘The Right to be Forgotten – The Law and Practical Issues’ by Melissa Stock |
| ‘A Practical Guide to Planning Law and Rights of Way in National Parks, the Broads and AONBs’ by James Maurici QC, James Neill et al |
| ‘A Practical Guide to Election Law’ by Tom Tabori |
| ‘A Practical Guide to the Law in Relation to Surrogacy’ by Andrew Powell |
| ‘A Practical Guide to Claims Arising from Fatal Accidents – 2nd Edition’ by James Patience |
| ‘A Practical Guide to the Ownership of Employee Inventions – From Entitlement to Compensation’ by James Tumbridge & Ashley Roughton |
| ‘A Practical Guide to Asbestos Claims’ by Jonathan Owen & Gareth McAloon |
| ‘A Practical Guide to Stamp Duty Land Tax in England and Northern Ireland’ by Suzanne O’Hara |
| ‘A Practical Guide to the Law of Farming Partnerships’ by Philip Whitcomb |
| ‘Covid-19, Homeworking and the Law – The Essential Guide to Employment and GDPR Issues’ by Forbes Solicitors |
| ‘Covid-19 and Criminal Law – The Essential Guide’ by Ramya Nagesh |

| |
|---|
| 'Covid-19 and Family Law in England and Wales – The Essential Guide' by Safda Mahmood |
| 'A Practical Guide to the Law of Unlawful Eviction and Harassment – 2nd Edition' by Stephanie Lovegrove |
| 'Covid-19, Brexit and the Law of Commercial Leases – The Essential Guide' by Mark Shelton |
| 'A Practical Guide to Costs in Personal Injury Claims – 2nd Edition' by Matthew Hoe |
| 'A Practical Guide to the General Data Protection Regulation (GDPR) – 2nd Edition' by Keith Markham |
| 'Ellis on Credit Hire – Sixth Edition' by Aidan Ellis & Tim Kevan |
| 'A Practical Guide to Working with Litigants in Person and McKenzie Friends in Family Cases' by Stuart Barlow |
| 'Protecting Unregistered Brands: A Practical Guide to the Law of Passing Off' by Lorna Brazell |
| 'A Practical Guide to Secondary Liability and Joint Enterprise Post-Jogee' by Joanne Cecil & James Mehigan |
| 'A Practical Guide to the Pre-Action RTA Claims Protocol for Personal Injury Lawyers' by Antonia Ford |
| 'A Practical Guide to Neighbour Disputes and the Law' by Alexander Walsh |
| 'A Practical Guide to Forfeiture of Leases' by Mark Shelton |
| 'A Practical Guide to Coercive Control for Legal Practitioners and Victims' by Rachel Horman |
| 'Tackling Disclosure in the Criminal Courts – A Practitioner's Guide' by Narita Bahra QC & Don Ramble |
| 'A Practical Guide to the Law of Driverless Cars – Second Edition' by Alex Glassbrook, Emma Northey & Scarlett Milligan |
| 'A Practical Guide to TOLATA Claims' by Greg Williams |
| 'A Practical Guide to Elderly Law – 2nd Edition' by Justin Patten |
| 'A Practical Guide to Responding to Housing Disrepair and Unfitness Claims' by Iain Wightwick |
| 'A Practical Guide to the Law of Bullying and Harassment in the Workplace' by Philip Hyland |
| 'How to Be a Freelance Solicitor: A Practical Guide to the SRA-Regulated Freelance Solicitor Model' by Paul Bennett |
| 'A Practical Guide to Prison Injury Claims' by Malcolm Johnson |

| |
|---|
| 'A Practical Guide to the Small Claims Track – 2nd Edition' by Dominic Bright |
| 'A Practical Guide to Advising Clients at the Police Station' by Colin Stephen McKeown-Beaumont |
| 'A Practical Guide to Antisocial Behaviour Injunctions' by Iain Wightwick |
| 'Practical Mediation: A Guide for Mediators, Advocates, Advisers, Lawyers, and Students in Civil, Commercial, Business, Property, Workplace, and Employment Cases' by Jonathan Dingle with John Sephton |
| 'The Mini-Pupillage Workbook' by David Boyle |
| 'A Practical Guide to Crofting Law' by Brian Inkster |
| 'A Practical Guide to the Law of Domain Names and Cybersquatting' by Andrew Clemson |
| 'A Practical Guide to the Law of Gender Pay Gap Reporting' by Harini Iyengar |
| 'NHS Whistleblowing and the Law' by Joseph England |
| 'Employment Law and the Gig Economy' by Nigel Mackay & Annie Powell |
| 'A Practical Guide to Noise Induced Hearing Loss (NIHL) Claims' by Andrew Mckie, Ian Skeate, Gareth McAloon |
| 'An Introduction to Beauty Negligence Claims – A Practical Guide for the Personal Injury Practitioner' by Greg Almond |
| 'Intercompany Agreements for Transfer Pricing Compliance' by Paul Sutton |
| 'Zen and the Art of Mediation' by Martin Plowman |
| 'A Practical Guide to the SRA Principles, Individual and Law Firm Codes of Conduct 2019 – What Every Law Firm Needs to Know' by Paul Bennett |
| 'A Practical Guide to Adoption for Family Lawyers' by Graham Pegg |
| 'A Practical Guide to Industrial Disease Claims' by Andrew Mckie & Ian Skeate |
| 'A Practical Guide to Redundancy' by Philip Hyland |
| 'A Practical Guide to Vicarious Liability' by Mariel Irvine |
| 'A Practical Guide to Applications for Landlord's Consent and Variation of Leases' by Mark Shelton |
| 'A Practical Guide to Relief from Sanctions Post-Mitchell and Denton' by Peter Causton |
| 'A Practical Guide to Equity Release for Advisors' by Paul Sams |
| 'A Practical Guide to Financial Services Claims' by Chris Hegarty |
| 'The Law of Houses in Multiple Occupation: A Practical Guide to HMO Proceedings' by Julian Hunt |

| |
|---|
| 'Occupiers, Highways and Defective Premises Claims: A Practical Guide Post-Jackson – 2nd Edition' by Andrew Mckie |
| 'A Practical Guide to Financial Ombudsman Service Claims' by Adam Temple & Robert Scrivenor |
| 'A Practical Guide to Running Housing Disrepair and Cavity Wall Claims: 2nd Edition' by Andrew Mckie & Ian Skeate |
| 'A Practical Guide to Holiday Sickness Claims – 2nd Edition' by Andrew Mckie & Ian Skeate |
| 'Arguments and Tactics for Personal Injury and Clinical Negligence Claims' by Dorian Williams |
| 'A Practical Guide to Drone Law' by Rufus Ballaster, Andrew Firman, Eleanor Clot |
| 'A Practical Guide to Compliance for Personal Injury Firms Working With Claims Management Companies' by Paul Bennett |
| 'RTA Allegations of Fraud in a Post-Jackson Era: The Handbook – 2nd Edition' by Andrew Mckie |
| 'RTA Personal Injury Claims: A Practical Guide Post-Jackson' by Andrew Mckie |
| 'On Experts: CPR35 for Lawyers and Experts' by David Boyle |
| 'An Introduction to Personal Injury Law' by David Boyle |

www.ingramcontent.com/pod-product-compliance
Lightning Source LLC
LaVergne TN
LVHW022042200926
848481LV00003B/752
*9781916698246*